Selected mountain bike rides in M

First Edition

By

Chris Lazenby

Kate Long

Sue Savege

Design

Bikefax

Illustrations

Christopher Havill

Published by Bikefax Ltd. North Wales. UK. www.bike-fax.com

ISBN: 0-9549762-5-8

Cover photo:
Route: Les Gets 2
Rider: Chris Lazenby
Photographer: Danny Crofts

This book includes mapping data licensed from IGN®

Publisher's note:

Mountain bike routes are subject to the forces of both nature and man, and can change on a day to day basis. Every effort has been made in putting together this book to check routes and ensure the accuracy of the mapping. But beware rain can wash out the trail, forest routes can come and go and routes seem to get harder or easier in direct proportion to the time spent in the saddle. Make sure you are ready for your day out in the dirt and check out the latest updates on access and trail conditions at www.bike-fax.com.

Contents

After many an awesome summer spent working and riding in Portes du Soleil, we went out this year and rode as many trails as we could to put together this book, and to help you enjoy the riding experience without needing to wonder or worry about where to go.

The journey into Portes du Soleil gives you an idea of the scale of the mountains you are heading to. They're not the higher Alps but in comparison to anything we have in the UK, the length of descents possible here must be seen to be believed. The atmosphere here is fully outdoor friendly, with the French/Swiss angle on a healthy, active life. If you like your steak and salads, food is amazing and if you like stringy cheeses, you'll be in heaven.

You'll go up on hugely steep chair li[f] see ridiculously long zip cord rides, fir a village populated by goats, feel yc leg muscles burning and all your bon jangling, as you plummet down steep slopes than you ever imagined you'd ri in your life, and all the time have a big g plastered over your face.

Portes du Soleil is home to so m[a] adventure sports and activities, you'll hard pushed to find nothing to do duri[ng] your visit. There's rally, 4x4 motor sp horse riding, golf, tennis, Luge, Devalk swimming, water sports, paraglid[ing] climbing (via ferrate), road biking (Tour France stages) as well as mountain bik in all shapes and sizes.

We love it here and you'll find us most summer evenings at the Boomerang Hotel and most days on a bike heading downhill or over the tops to Switzerland.

To cover the total of over 300 mountain bike trails in the whole of this region of the lower Alps would turn this guide into a huge encyclopaedia, so we have concentrated on the areas with the largest range to suit all, plus a few of the less visited areas, for those who like to explore further afield.

Have a great time wearing yourself out on these fantastic trails, we'll see you this summer!

Additional…

In general, the severity of the trails in the alpine areas will be of a more demanding nature than those you ride back home.

For you DH guys it's 'every man for themselves'. Just go and 'have it' but please remember to respect other newer/slower riders and pedestrians in order to avoid conflict, which can lead to closure of trails just like in the UK.

Never fully attack a trail until you have ridden it a few times as there may be something lurking round the corner.

Even though this book is written with detail and accuracy in mind, sometimes things change that are unavoidable. Every now and then the courses change which is down to weather or are re-directed due to maintenance. Please take care, and do not assume that what was there last year will be there again today!

Grade assessments:

Please Note:

As this is the first book which includes downhill specific riding we have set up a new grading system which is based on riding the DH trails at average ride speeds including those XC riders giving them a fair go. This means the grade may be read as harder or easier depending on your abilities.

If you like this guide book, we will be looking at producing further detail to the Portes du Soleil in more specific guides in the future. So if you have any requests or have any comments about the guides we produce, please contact us through the web site. We aim to produce precise and useful information so any input you give will be taken into account for future productions.

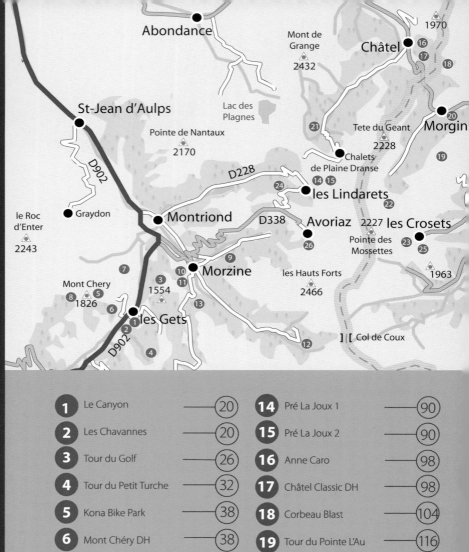

Abondance

Mont de Grange
△ 2432

Châtel ● △ 1970
16
17
18

St-Jean d'Aulps ●

Lac des Plagnes

Morgin ● 20

19

Pointe de Nantaux
△ 2170

D902

Tete du Geant
△ 2228

21

Chalets de Plaine Dranse ●

D228

24 14 15

Graydon ●

le Roc d'Enter
△ 2243

les Lindarets ●
22

Montriond ●

D338

Avoriaz ● 2227 les Crosets
△   △

Pointe des Mossettes
△

23
25

26

7

9

△ 1963

Mont Chery
△ 1826

8   5

3
1554 △

10

Morzine ●

les Hauts Forts
△ 2466

6

11

13

] | [Col de Coux

1 les Gets ●

2

D902

4

12

Introduction

The towns of Morzine and Les Gets in the Portes du Soleil region of the French Alps, are two of the most vibrant summer mountain biking venues in Europe.

Located in the Northern French Alps just south of Lake Geneva, the area manages to combine fantastic scenery and a favourable climate with a host of both built and natural trails plus a lively après-bike scene. In short, it's the perfect mountain biking holiday venue!

With 660km of winter ski and snowboard pistes metamorphosing into hundreds of kilometres of amazing multi-graded freeride, downhill and cross country trails, there's something for everyone, be they families or DH adrenalin junkies.

The Portes du Soleil kicks off it's biking season with a community mass bike ride called the 'Tour des Portes du Soleil'.

This tour takes in over 200km of trails around the region's circumference. Now that's bike mad!

Most years, the small towns of Les Gets and Morzine are host to World Cup and National mountain bike races. With professional 4X, DH, XC and trials riders pounding the tracks, time it right, and there is full exciting action for all to see.

If you're into downhilling or just need a rest from the steep ups, then using the télésiège lifts gives you access to most peaks and helps to supply seemingly never ending energy!

There is a large downhill element to the area but if you are a technically competent cross country rider, don't be afraid to try these trails. You can ride most of the routes with a normal full suspension bike, just make sure you keep aware of other riders and hop out of the way of the faster riders if you do have to pause for breath.

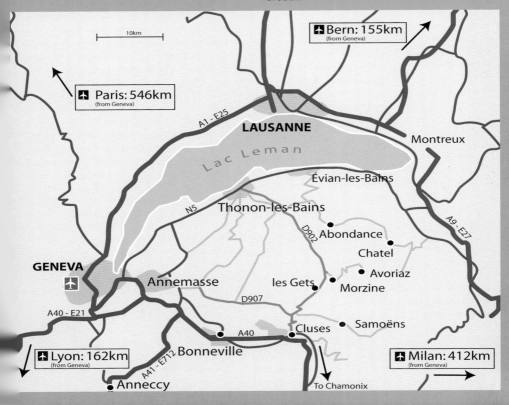

For all riders, crossing the French/Swiss border is another buzz to be had, making you feel like you're on an expedition not just a mountain bike ride.

Long cross country outings have you crossing and re-crossing the border between the two countries, while for the downhiller, a trip to the superb Swiss National course just over the border at Les Crosets, is a must.

In the Portes du Soleil the biking community really comes into it's own. You can get out and explore cross country before après-ride beers at 6pm.

Alternatively, have a long late breakfast, head straight for some of the best down hill tracks in the world and just nail those trails until you either run out of steam or the lifts shut!

Getting there

Portes du Soleil is 590km from Paris and 1000km from London.

If you do decide to drive, the long trek can pay off as you'll have the freedom to explore the whole region to the full. Driving is quite an arduous event and best shared between at least two to avoid being too tired to get on your bike on arrival.

Travelling overland can be a cheaper option too, especially if there is a group of you but don't forget to take road tolls into account and any expenses for a stopover you may decide on to split the journey.

There are many Novotels along the route and some lovely bed and breakfasts if you go into the towns you pass by. Hotels enroute to the Portes du Soleil are nationally classified from A to I. A grade is the cheapest at about £45 for a double room B&B per night.

Don't forget your driving time and fuel economy is affected if you have the bike packed on the outside of the vehicle and allow for this in your driving time.

Driving distances and routes can be checked at: www.viamichelin.com.

Airports

Geneva is the nearest airport with flights from most main British or European airports arriving several times a day during the holiday season. Flying is a convenient option especially with Easyjet charging just £10.00 each way at present for a bike in box or bag.

Check with airlines that it's okay to bring a bike with your luggage as they may turn it down or charge you an arm and a leg if you don't pre-book. There are also weight restrictions and over-weight luggage can have additional payments per kilo demanded so pack your weight within reason.

If you travel by Easyjet, remember to take your flight reference with you and keep it safe for your return as they now have automated baggage tagging for flights out of Geneva.

You can also sort out or pick up your hire car at the airport and most accommodation providers will give a transfer booking service. Just make sure you give them the correct flight details to avoid any confusion.

For more travel information:
www.viamichelin.com
www.seafrance.com
www.flybe.com
www.poferries.com
www.flybmi.com
www.airfrance.com
www.flyglobespan.com
www.openjet.com
www.eurotunnel.com
www.easyjet.com
www.brittanyferries.com

Local Cuisine

If you're staying in half or full board accommodation, there is usually a high standard of service from the kitchen staff and chef(s) in charge. Most catered meals will include at least two courses plus a bread basket topped up throughout the meal. Wine is usually extra in catered accommodation. A favourite in the winter season; the cheese fondue is a fun meal to share and available from most restaurants.

Being a region renowned for its stringy melted cheeses there is never a shortage of hot Raclette which you can get in baguettes from bakeries and many small cafes around the area.

If you're partial to a steak make sure to try them while you're here as you'll usually get a better than average platefull compared to the UK. But just remember, if you don't like it fully bloody in the middle ask for it: 'tres bien qui' (very well done).

In most of the popular biking areas, if you're after a quick lunch ready for the afternoon ride, you can easily find small street-side cafes.

These are readily visible near the bottom of lifts and most allow you to park your bike up by your table while you grab a mountain style hot dog or burger with French fries and a bottled or canned drink. Even the smallest village will have an eatery; just make sure you don't turn up to a sit-down restaurant with a totally muddy bum!

You can also buy stocks for lunches on wheels from the town markets where they sell amazing local produce including cheeses, preserved sausages and fresh vegetables as well as all kinds of sea food and bread. There are small supermarkets in most towns which stock plenty of munchies.

Accommodation

Keeping in harmony with the local Alpine environment and rural farmlands, many hotels and chalets are wood and stone built. Generally apartments and chalets for rent will have one living space with sitting area, kitchen and, if you're lucky, a balcony.

You'll generally be able to get reasonably priced accommodation which fits more people than there are bedrooms as most come with extra sleeping facilities in the form of pull out settees and twin beds.

Check what's available before you go as adding one person to the group can save you a fair bit of money so long as you don't mind squashing in.

There are so many places to stay in the region that it would be impossible to list them. Many people opt to stay in Morzine or Les Gets as this puts you right in the heart of all that is so attractive about the area. Alternatively you can stay in or around Avoriaz or in the Châtel Valley.

Wherever you decide to stay, just type mountain biking and the village of your choice into a search engine and a whole heap of options will come up. Have a look at the section introductions for more specific information.

Weather Information

The mountains of Morzine and the Portes du Soleil are not as high as those in neighbouring Chamonix and Mont Blanc, and as such the area doesn't attract quite so much of the stormy alpine weather more familiar in the higher alps.

From June through to September you can expect it to be pleasantly warm, usually riding in just a long sleeved top. Being in the mountains though, you might not escape the rain altogether, so its still worth taking a waterproof top. Alternatively you could be like the locals, and just not go out in the rain at all!!

www.meteo.fr
www.theweathernetwork.com

Local Guides and MTB Operators

There is a whole host of guiding and holiday companies operating in the Portes du Soleil. Once in the area, a visit to the local Guides Bureau, the local Tourist Information Office or one of the local bike shops will point you in the direction of local ride guides.

Have a look at the section introductions for more specific information on this.

Similarly a trawl through the internet or the back of the MTB mags will bring up a list of operators in the area. Then its simply a matter of whittling them down to the ones you like the look of.

Useful Contacts for holidays and guiding:

Association Internationale des Portes d Soleil, 1401 Route de Vonnes F-74 390 Châte

www.portesdusoleil.com

www.alpinetracks.co.uk

www.rideontours.co.uk

www.leboomerang.com

www.alpinepursuits.com

www.mountainbikeholidays.co.uk

www.peakretreats.co.uk

www.challenge-activ.com

www.morzinelets.com

More biking info

The Federtion Francaise de Cyclisme (FFC has information on VTT (Velo Tout Terrain sites around the country. They also produce series of leaflets on VTT routes which you ca usually pick up at the Office de Tourisme

www.ffc.fr

Insurance

This is a must for this type of activity holiday.

Speaking from experience, if you have a major injury and require medi-vacing home or operation(s), your E111 will only cover a percentage of the costs and the less stress the better at times like that so come prepared. You can get an E111 which entitles you to a certain amount of medical treatment in the European Union from any Post Office .

You may also want to take travel insurance just in case the love of your life (no not the spouse – your bike) gets nicked or seriously broken. But only specialist policies are likely to be any use for a mountain biking trip.

For insurance info:

www.sportscoverdirect.com

www.snowcard.co.uk

Please note, although you may see a rescue helicopter, it may not be able to access all areas so make sure someone back at your holiday resort knows where you're riding and when to expect you to return.

Emergency numbers are to be used ONLY in case of emergency or as in the UK you will find yourself ending up being slapped with a huge bill.

Local Hospitals

Thonon Les Bains\Evian tel: 0450832000
Monthey (Switzerland) 00 41244731731
Geneva (Switzerland) 00 413823311
No d'urgence:
Landline 15 (like our 999)
Mobile 112

How to use this guide

As mountain bikers, we've often thought about what we would want from a guidebook ourselves. We all know how difficult it is to turn up in a brand new area and not know quite where to start, hence this guide. With the help of local riders, we've done some of the work for you, checking out the local services and riding the trails with notebook, camera and GPS, to put together the best information possible.

To make it easy for riders to choose the right route, the routes have been arranged by geographic area, with each area then giving a selection of both downhill and cross country routes at a variety of grades. If you want to find all the downhill, cross country, epics etc in the region, have a look at the 'Graded List' at the back of the book.

Maps & Symbols

The maps used in this guide are based on standard IGN mapping. The maps have been redrawn to highlight the most important information whilst giving mountain bike riders additional detail to help with getting the most out of the ride.

Whilst we have made every effort to check the accuracy of our maps, there are times when only a full detailed map will do and for the longer, more remote rides we strongly recommend that you take a map and compass with you- and know how to use them!

Icons

The icons on the map should give you extra information about the nature of the trail, as well as the location of any amenities you might find on route.

Gradings explained

The gradings in this book are here for you to decide what's your own poison: ride with the challenge of never 'dabbing'; push yourself on something a little harder than usual, or stay well within your comfort zone.

This guide contains both purpose built 'Downhill' (DH) tracks and classic 'Cross-Country' (XC) rides.

Level of Difficulty

Downhill routes are given a technical grade from 1 – 5 to indicate their level of severity and technical difficulty.

It is notoriously hard to grade the level of difficulty of mountain bike routes. So much will depend on you, the bike and the conditions on the day. As well as this, the level of difficulty of a route can change from year to year, as tracks get washed out by the rain, maintained or rebuilt. In this book we attempt to give you some guide as to the level of the hardest riding to expect on each route.

Downhill Routes - DH

The higher the grade: the harder the route. All this means higher grades equal bigger jumps, steeper inclines and more demanding technical sections.

 Easy

Straightforward off-road riding, forest roads and wide grassy tracks. All you need is some knobbly tyres on your bike and you can go for it. Suitable for all including novices and children.

Moderate

Wide bumpy trails with a choice of lines, simple singletrack, moderate inclines and nothing too technical.

3 Hard

Fast flowing singletrack, with generally good traction on the surface. Good bike control needed and some quick decision making. Expect variable surfaces from smooth hardpack to loose rock, mud and roots. Small jumps and rollers.

4 Extreme

Technically challenging riding with tight switchbacks, narrow rutted tracks and loose surfaces. Fast riding with jumps, steep inclines and obstacles all around you. Riding where expert bike control is essential and good balance at a premium. At least wear elbow and shin pads on this stuff.

5 Off the Scale

Big jumps, scary landings, impossible surfaces and split second decision making. You'll most likely be wearing full body armour for this stuff. Limited or no chicken runs here. Routes for those who 'have it' on a regular or competition basis.

If you don't find these rides hard – turn pro!

Cross Country Rides - XC

Cross-Country rides use a dual grading system to indicate both the nature of the ride and the hardest level of technical difficulty which you are likely to encounter. First; grades from Epic to Family give you an overall impression of the route, then numeric 1 – 5 grades give you an idea of the technical difficulty of the ride. Put the two gradings together, for example, Expert 3 to get the real impression what to expect on a cross country ride.

 Epic

Epic routes as the name implies contain serious sections of downhill for long periods of time, thigh-ripping technical uphill and some severe endurance issues!. Go prepared as anything can come at you at anytime.

Expert

Almost wholly off road. You'll need a reasonable level of fitness and a fair bit of experience on a bike. Riding on these trails can be of a challenging nature and you'll be trying your best not to fall off.

Classic

With big sweeping views and good distance coverage these rides can take you far from the beaten track. Classic routes will appeal to the rider who wants to cover the miles, see the scenery and enjoy the ride.

Blasts

Great routes for blowing away the cobwebs when you've only got an hour or so to spare or for when the weather is being particularly ugly in the mountains. These routes offer a quick up and down, but don't underestimate them, some of these little routes can pack a powerful punch.

Family

Mountain biking isn't just for the grown ups, start 'em young and get the kids out on the bikes too. Family rides combine short easy rides with an element of fun. Easy riding on wide tracks mean that these routes are just as suitable for novices as they are for the kids.

Kit and Equipment

What to wear & what to take with you.

Cross Country

IIf you're going off the beaten track or into the high mountains, it's a good idea to take a few extra bits with you.

- Spare food
- Spare clothing
- Bothy bag/emergency shelter
- First Aid
- Hydration
- Couple of spare tubes each
- Repair kit/Multi-tool
- Zip Ties & Gaffer tape (you can temporarily fix just about anything with these)
- Mobile Phone - Be aware that you may not be able to get a signal some places
- A well maintained bike

  Give your bike a once over before starting. Make sure the essentials are well lubed and the brakes are working properly

The list of kit for cross country riding in the French Alps differs little from riding at home - a few handy extras though

- Plenty of euros for all the enroute cafes and mountain huts
- A larger than normal camelback or similar
- Local map and compass

Downhill

If you haven't been before and intend throwing yourself straight into the rush of the 'downhill'. Make sure you think about the kit you should have before heading off.

You'll most likely be going downhill pretty steeply and, pretty fast, often through some very tight tree sections on these routes, so we recommend that you pad yourself up as well as possible.

Recommended DH kit:

- Full gloves
- Full face helmet (never go on DH trails without at least a normal mtb helmet)
- Long sleeves
- Full Body armour if you've got it
- Elbow guards
- Knee and shin pads at least
- Backguard, ideally
- If you're new to DH you might prefer flat pedals to make a quick exit easier.
- Chainguard (to protect your bike)

Code of Conduct & Rules of the Trail

General common sense applies here of course. The age-old rule of 'show consideration to others and they'll be considerate to you', works on the whole. For all the times that this doesn't work, a basic minimum of politeness should at least mean that we present a positive image of our sport.

- Always ride on legal trails.
- Leave no trace.
- Be sensitive to the soil beneath you and practice low-impact cycling. Wet and muddy trails are more vulnerable to damage, so when the trail is soft, consider riding alternative trails.
- Stay in control of your bike.
- Judge when it is appropriate to ride fast so as to avoid incidents with others.
- Always give way to faster riders on DH. On XC give way to riders coming up the hill.
- Let your fellow trail users know you're coming. Anticipate other trail users around corners or in blind spots.
- Never Scare Animals. This can be dangerous for you, others, and the animals, so give animals extra room and time to adjust to you.
- Leave gates as you found them, or as marked.
- Plan ahead and be self sufficient. A well-executed trip is a satisfaction to you and not a burden to others. Carry some spares, as well as some food and first aid.

If you do come off your bike or have to pause for breath – make sure you move yourself and your bike well to the side of the trail to avoid someone ploughing into the back of you.

Emergency Procedures

If it does all go horribly wrong and someone in your group ends up in a big bloody pile on the floor, then this is where all that extra stuff comes in handy. First of all make sure your casualty and everyone else for that matter stays warm, get him or her in to shelter and patch 'em up if you can.

If they're too crook to walk out, it's probably time to call for some professional help. If you are in the forest, they might be able to get the ambulance to you, anything more remote than this and it's probably going to be a job for the Mountain Rescue.

The number to call from your mobile is 112, ask for the police, explain your situation, try to tell them exactly where you are and the nature of the injuries, and they will then call the appropriate services. Remember to keep your phone on after this, as they will need to get back to you for more details.

Then sit back and wait; it could easily be a couple of hours before someone can get help to you.

The moral of the story is **RIDE SAFE**, take plenty of kit and don't crash and burn.

8

Mont Caly

Pointe de la Turche

Les Gets

Mont Chéry

les Gets

les Chavannes

D902

Pointe de Nyon

Introduction

Fast becoming a summer home for many a british rider, Les Gets has been host to both World Cup and World Championship XC and DH competitions.

Discovering Les Gets means letting the tradition that built the village guide you, letting yourself be seduced by the charm of the authentic chalets, finding again the feeling of freedom. If we attempted to describe the atmosphere in the village, we would say that there exists a mountain biking spirit, a soul flowing above this little corner of paradise, situated between Lake Geneva and Mont Blanc.

For many travellers from the UK, Les Chavannes and the Mont Chéry DH trails at Les Gets will be the first stopping off point on their tour of the Portes du Soleil. This small town makes it very easy to just get on your bike and ride, and once you've had a couple of days here, you'll no doubt be graduating on to harder grades very quickly.

This is where all the riding hotshots stay to train in the summer, so don't be surprised to have some international star tearing up the trail in front of you. Just watch and learn!

Getting there

From Paris -

If you're driving down from the Paris direction get on the A6 towards Macon Nord, then Anemasse and finally the A40 to Cluses. At Cluses the motorway ends and you travel into the mountains on the D902 to Les Gets

From Geneva -

If you've flown in and hired a car at the airport, take the A40 to Cluses. At Cluses get onto the D902 to Les Gets.

Local services

In the way of bike shops there are couple of half-ski, half-bike shops that may have the part you are after, but it is a bit of a gamble. To stand a better chance of finding stuff, head to 'Evasion', nestled between Bar Bush and the Mont Chéry lift. This underground shop carries most of the things you could want.

Food, drink and sleep

Les Gets is a village based around tourism, both in winter and in summer, and as such there are no end of places to eat. Rather than list them all, have the fun in wandering around and trying them for yourself.

You can get a taste of home at the English owned Bar Bush in the middle of town. On the other side of town and just on the main road to Morzine, the very well known Hotel Le Boomerang is the place of choice for après bike drinking and general socialising. They have a great restaurant as well as bar snacks such as Nachos or Fries. Great place to hang out and get plenty of local ride information, and in the evenings get your bike serviced here by Ride On.

In the centre of town, you can choose from traditional and excellent French fare, pizza or patisserie; all are excellent and friendly.

The accommodation situation is the same as finding somewhere to eat. There are small collection of contacts listed below, but for a complete listing visit the Les Gets website.

Useful contacts

Camping: La Grange Au Frene

www.ride-ontours.co.uk

www.lesgets.com

www.hotel-nagano.com

www.alpensport-hotel.com

www.peakretreats.co.uk

www.alpinepursuits.com

www.leboomerang.com

B+B: Chalet L'Envala

chalet.lenvala@libertysurf.fr

Le Canyon / Les Chavannes

Les Gets

Getting There

Head down the main shopping street, away from Morzine. Shortly after the Casino supermarket on the left, turn left, opposite the Shopi supermarket. If you are feeling hungry at this point, stop for a quick hot dog / kebab at kiosk on the right, halfway down the street. At the T-junction, turn left (one way street). Almost immediately turn right up a stepped path towards the lift station.

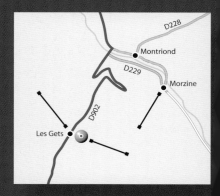

Start Points

On exiting the top lift station the start of the Chavanne is to your right.

To get to Le Canyon go left down the road for 200m until you see a path sign posted off left, head down here into the trees.

Le Canyon

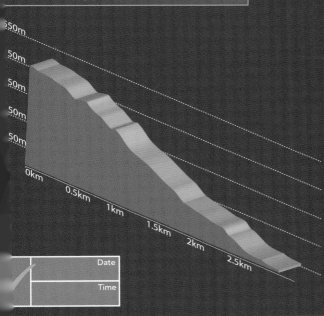

550m
500m
450m
400m
350m

0km
0.5km
1km
1.5km
2km
2.5km

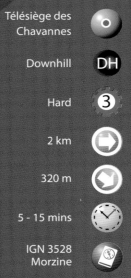

Télésiège des Chavannes

Downhill DH

Hard ③

2 km

320 m

5 - 15 mins

IGN 3528 Morzine

	Date
	Time

Les Chavannes

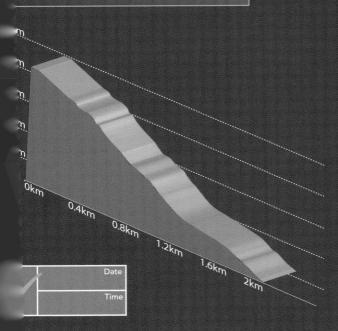

0km
0.4km
0.8km
1.2km
1.6km
2km

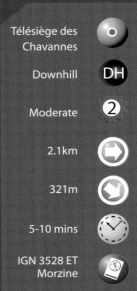

Télésiège des Chavannes

Downhill DH

Moderate ②

2.1km

321m

5-10 mins

IGN 3528 ET Morzine

	Date
	Time

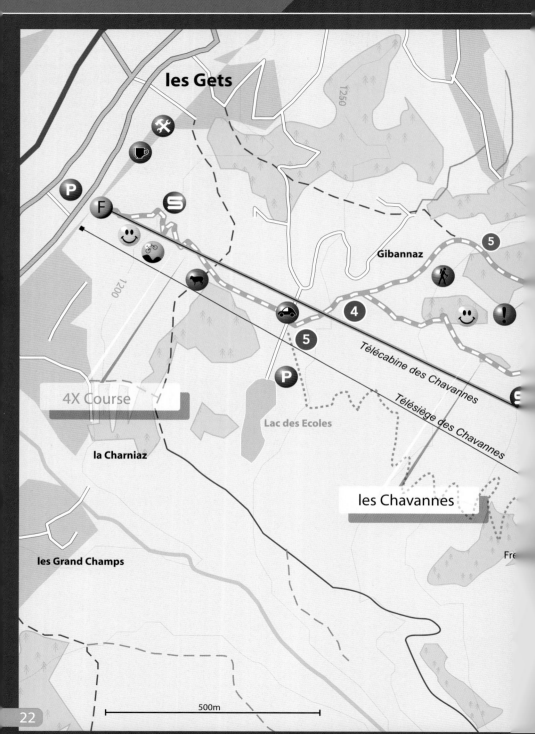

les Gets

Gibannaz

Télécabine des Chavannes

Télésiège des Chavannes

4X Course

Lac des Ecoles

les Chavannes

la Charniaz

les Grand Champs

Fre

500m

le Canyon

1400

3

2

!

2

!

1

S

1484

S

P

1

les Chavannes

1500

DH Summary: Le Canyon

The Gully run or Canyon is a relatively short tra, but is littered with many variations down the same run. The name of the run gives away its most appealing feature, narrow gullies. Although these gullies only occupy a part of the track, it is these sections that stick in your mind.

This track is mostly made up of fast, very rooty sections interspersed with the odd little jump and drop. Regardless of your chosen steed this is a track that needs attention, and best avoided by the wary hard tail rider.

DH Summary: Les Chavannes

At just 2.1 kilometres, the Chavanne Downhill Course is only short, but it is nevertheless one of the most enjoyable of the less demanding tracks in the area. The Chavanne makes a great warm up route if you've just arrived in the area.

As it is only graded 'french blue', there are no particularly steep or technical sections to the route so you have plenty of time to tweak both bike and body ready for some of the more technical tracks around.

DH Le Canyon

1 Fast Single Track

The start of the run is very fast singletrack aided by a good run in from the road, beware a small drop-in when first entering the trail. After around a hundred metres the roots start. Either attack these at full speed and bounce over the top or go more steady and pick a smoother line. Through a few trees then out into the open briefly for some nice short singletrack. Caution!

2 The Gully

The gully starts here. You need to scrub off speed before entering the gully as you are immediately faced with small, tight drops littered with hundreds of roots. After a short gully section the trail forks into 2 separate tracks. Both fun but quite different. The right hand one is one trail that tacks in a big corner, lots of roots and a small gully section. But joins in with the main trail later on. The left hand track is the one described here, as it is generally believed to be more fun.

3 Deeper Gully

Carry on down through a deeper gully, when faced with lots of little different lines, keep to the left. They all link up but the right hand side leads to a really tight rooty section with a big drop to the right. Take care through this section as the trail undulates a lot with a large amount of weight shifting to be done. When the trail heads down into a small narrow compression and back up round a tight tree – caution! This next shoot needs to be tackled with full concentration and commitment. Off camber roots on steep bank offer many a rider a chance to be on the deck. Get to the bottom round another tight tree, down a small bank and through little stream. Low gear needed here, as small amount of pedalling is required to get up a little slope to the next section.

4 Stump Drop

After coming up the slope and round the corner, the trail leads round to the left. Keep to the right before turning and swing round late to do the stump drop. It's an awkward one because of the roots but it feels good when dialled. This is where the other track from before meets up. Pick up plenty of speed round the next steepish slope but beware of the super tight gully section coming up. Through there and onto a fast flatish slightly rutted section, fastest line to the left.

5 Wettish Section

Now the only real slow part of the track, lots of different routes to choose from. If wet this section can be awkward but in the dry the routes in the middle usually work the best. To stay with the gully keep to the right at the next fork, this just gets faster and faster till you shoot out the end into the open and joining the last section of Les Chavannes.

6 4X Track

Across the road and down the 4X track and you're back where you started. Now you know roughly what to expect you can tr some of the other variations. Enjoy!

DH Chavanne

1 Steep Sweeping Right Hander

The track starts with a quick open right-hander into a fairly tight high-banked left. There is then a short straight section, before floating over some roots and dropping into a super fast right hand berm.

Go over the jump on the exit and keep as low as possible to stay on the correct line. Then it's just a couple of nice berms and a flattish section through some trees and you are into section 2.

2 Tree Switchback

As you come out of the trees you soon pick up speed for the tight left-right kink into the technical part of the track. Another tight couple of corners on the exit and the track continues into the open with some flat out corners before going back into the trees for the third section.

3 Fast Step Down

This section starts with a short straight into a series of extremely tight right-left combinations. If you have kePt your speed, you are faced with a fast little straight to set you up for a fantastic step down into a narrow gully (chicken run to the right). Make the step down and you will now feel like the fastest person on the planet as you float over the roots. Watch out for a reasonably tight right-hander next (this can be done with no brakes but it's not advised first time round).

4 Field Section

The last section of the track is an open field with several flat out off camber corners. This part is all about line choice. Stay on the correct line and lay off the brakes to keep your speed for a fantastic finish.

5 Road and Car park

There are two ways to get back to the village: A) Follow the road to the right, at the junction take the left. Keep going down the hill back to the village.

Or for a bit more action

B) Go straight over the road and down the gravel track for around 100yds. At the trees follow the right path to lead you onto the old 4 Cross course.

4X Track

The 4X track starts by going down a wide trail for about 100m, then taking you into the trees through a rooty section and feeding you into a jump and a drop. After this short fast section you hop back up another little jump for a tight right hander with a high berm round to the right and then an even higher berm taking you back left.

After this there is a double step up into another berm taking you back right which now drops steeply down and back up with a great lift off. From here a very tight left hand turn drops you down the slope where you can pick up speed for a fast jump uphill. Here the trail levels out slightly but keep your speed for one final show-off step just before the track finishes back at the lift station.

bikefax

Tour du Golf

Les Gets

Summary

This is a great starter route for anyone new to riding in the lower Alps and also a great day out with the kids. The ride takes in some grand, rough singletrack along the ridge, includes short steep ups and downs running through to gravelled fire roads and then a final long sweeping grassy descent to get you back to Les Gets.

Not too long and not too technical, this short ride provides an ideal opportunity to develop bike handling skills. With the added bonus of fantastic views across to Mont Blanc, there are no shortage of great picnic spots either.

For the more experienced rider, the first half of the ride can be used as a link through from Les Gets to the top of the 'Avalanche Cup' downhill course at Morzine. The second half of the ride can then be used to get you back to Les Gets from Morzine without having to ride along the main road.

Télésiège des Chavannes

Family / Blast

Moderate 2

8 km

80 m

450 m

1-2 hrs

IGN 3528 Morzine

Getting There

To make it easy: take Les Chavannes Red Bubble to the top of the mountain. This lift is located in the centre of Les Gets on the East side of town. The lift's distinctive red bubbles can be seen above the 4 Cross trail at Les Chavannes. If you're driving into town, there are plenty of free parking areas not too far from the lift station. Park up and ride along the High Street until you see the lift station.

Start Point

When you exit the lift station you will see a tarmac road on your left. Turn left (East) and up the tarmac road. Just after the houses and restaurants of Les Chavannes you will see a wide worn singletrack in the grassy field up to your right. Look out for pedestrians (this trail is popular for walking as well as biking) and head upwards for a slow easy climb on a well worn track.

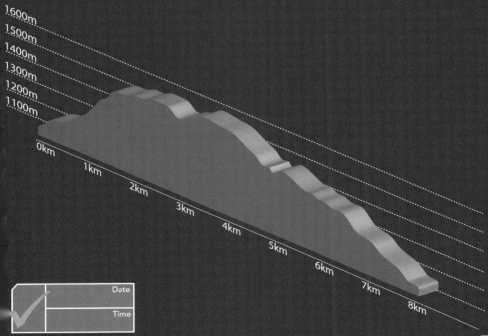

| Date |
| Time |

les Gets

les Chavannes

Télécabine des Chavannes

Télésiège des Chavannes

Golf Cou[r]

1490

D902

Ruisseau des Gets

1km

XC Tour du Golf

① VTT Post 3

Not far up the track you arrive at a VTT marker post 3, which states '2 hours to Morzine'. Here, in between trees, the track splits into two. Both routes continue to head along the ridge.

Choose either of the two tracks as they join up again after a short distance where the trail flattens out. Now there is an easy section with great views and picnic spots. Keep onward undulating up and down for a short distance.

② Short Rocky Downhill

Next is a short, steep and rocky downhill section. The track heads blindly around a corner where the rocks can be slippery in the wet and walkers can appear suddenly. Beware of both!

Use your speed at the bottom of the hill to charge you up the start of a short sharp steep section of uphill with a choice of very steep to the right and insanely steep to the left. This is a good exercise in preparation - being in the right gear is the key to success.

Fortunately this testing section is not very long and brings you gasping onto a trail to the right of the Golf Course.

3 Golf Course

Take a break now with an altogether more relaxing section of riding going along the flat to the clubhouse. The clubhouse has a wooden sculpture which looks like an advanced form of Jenga in front! You can take a rest here for a quick drink and take in what must be one of the most spectacular golfing views going.

Alternatively, head straight on to the right of the building and continue along a big gravel track. Shortly you come to a fork in the track. Here you can do a quick uphill sprint to a lookout point or go straight on, picking up a little speed as you do.

Keep going straight on as you control your speed whilst heading down to the top of the Morzine Plenay Lift.

4 Morzine Plenay Lift Station

Look to your left to follow the gravel fire road which continues running downhill. Follow this around a fast bend, to a short steep tarmac hill, controlling your speed as you do and looking out for pedestrians. This brings you to a small wooden hut on the lower side of the golf course where you can catch your breath for the run home.

5 Wooden Hut

Fly down a tarmac road now, checking your speed again on the corners, going around two sweeping bends, then a tight right hander. Look left now as you very quickly come to a wooden sign, often masked by long grass. This is where you need to turn off.

The route takes you up a very short uphill bit of singletrack then on to the flat for a moment before it's all downhill to home.

6 Singletrack

Check out a small wall ride to your left, then look ahead down the lovely singletrack to spot a small jump before a little wooden bridge over a brook. After this you wonder where the trail goes until you spot it running through a concrete tunnel to your right. This pops you out on to fantastic fast grassy singletrack where you can let the brakes off (looking out for a couple of drainage gullies) and head downward.

Look out for the exit of the Gully Run DH to your left as you flow along the off camber grassy trail. Check to your left for fast riders again as you follow the VTT tape on to the bottom of the Chavannes DH. This brings you over an often muddy stretch down to a tarmac road.

7 Tarmac Road & Car Park

There are two choices here for how to get back down to Les Gets here :

Either:

Turn right and follow the tarmac road right back into town

OR:

Head across the small car park and take in a few jumps and berms in the 4 Cross Area bringing you back to the bottom of the Red Bubbles lift station.

Optional Extras:

If you feel like a little extra riding you can add in a bit extra and even join it up with the Tour du Petite Turche. If you're planning on joing it up with the Tour du Golf, it's worth doing this bit at the beginning, thereby saving the best bit of downhill till last!!

Time: 30-45mins

Grade: Difficult

Summary: boggy sections, mainly fire road with lots of uphill burn.

Distance: 3km

Ascent: 260m

1 Follow the road from the bottom of the Chavannes DH trail toward the Lac for a very short distance until you see a small set of dirt jumps to your left. This is part of a previous XC World Championships track.

2 Turn up this singletrack which takes you into the woods and uphill over rough and often boggy ground. Continue uphill tackling tricky terrain, where you may have to carry your bike in some sections, until you reach a fire road joining from the right. Turn left onto the fire roads upslope and continue up this getting your legs ready for a good hour of mainly uphill.

3 Follow on around several bends up through the woods until you come out into an open space by La Mouille Rond (Pt 1360m) before coming to a fork in the track. Bear to the left still heading uphill and feel your legs begin to burn as the trail takes a stiff turn round to your left.

4 This brings you parallel with another fire road which, after a last short steep rise, both bring you up to a wider gravel track. Here you can turn left for a swift run downhill back to the top Chavannes lift station if you've had enough.

To continue on for the Tour du Petit Turche, turn right for continued uphill, meeting point 2 of it's description after approximately 100m.

31

Summary

The Tour du Petit Turche rewards the adventurous rider who is prepared for a good uphill battle on fire tracks, with great singletrack and fantastic views of Mont Blanc. This trail takes you over the hill into a new valley and back round again to leave you with a stunning feeling of altitude and achievement.

For the most part the trail is well sign posted with VTT markers, and a simple local map from the Tourist Office can provide a little bit of extra VTT Tour information.

There are endless opportunities to go exploring on this side of the mountain. With an extensive network of paths and tracks in and out of woods and ridges you could easily ride all day. You'll need at least a local map and a compass with you and maybe even a GPS if you're not going to end up wandering in circles.

Chavannes	
Classic	
Moderate	
16 km	
550 m	
780 m	
2-3 hrs	
IGN 3528 Morzine	

xploring in areas like this you never know quite
hat you are going to find next, so be prepared
r a bit of everything and make sure you are self
ufficient.

Getting There

the centre of town is the Télécabine Les Chavannes.
nown locally as the 'Red Bubble', the Chavannes
t provides a traditional and at times interesting
de in a wonky fibreglass sphere. An experience not to be missed!

ake the lift up to the top of the hill and on exiting the station, roll down to the car park to the
ght of the road ahead.

r an alternative, harder start to this ride, see the Tour du Golf and its optional extras.

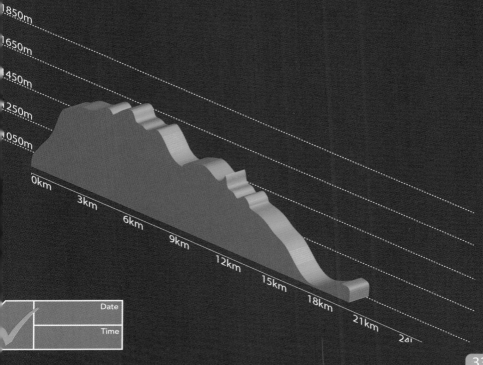

	Date
	Time

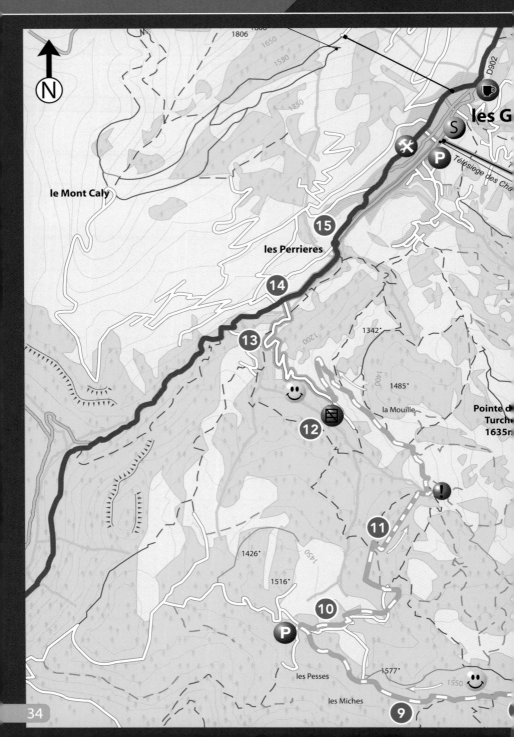

Tour du Petit Turche

1 Car Park

Turn right uphill out of the small car park at the top of the Chavannes lift. Stay on this gentle uphill track on a great packed gravel surface. Pass a signposted turn off to a trail on the right.

2 Track Junction

Come to a fork in the track at a sign for Les L'Hotels de Ranfolly. A wooden signpost pointing to the left, shows a yellow VTT No.6 marker. Follow the sign left onto a rough wide double track and pump slowly uphill.

3 VTT6

Keep heading up along signposted VTT6 yellow on wide singletrack shared with walkers. Take in amazing views and go over a cattle grid still heading uphill.

4 Signpost

Pass the signpost for Le Wetzet and continue up and up.

5 VTT Marker

At a way marker, turn right to join a flat gravel fire road heading east as it undulates down and up the hill.

6 Wooden Hut/ Mont Blanc Views

After a short distance look up left to a wooden hut where you will have an awesome glimpse of Mont Blanc as you continue going straight on uphill. Pass the colourful water butts on your left or stop for a quick drink (without being tempted to jump in one on a hot day!) and head up until you reach another VTT way marker.

7 Waymarker

Coming quickly to another way marker and take the left fork in the track for a last push up before topping out among a few trees and dropping down onto the rock strewn first bit of real descent. Enjoy the rest on your legs as you ride down a wide trail crossing some wooden sleepers over a muddy section.

8 La Mouille Nocher

Ride along a great rolling section in trees as you come round to the south side of the hill. At the next fork in the rough trail, go right, heading up to Point 1640m. This takes you up through la Mouille Nocher to more undulating track skirting in and out of the trees.

9 Woody Trail

Go right again at the next fork in the trail and head up again slightly through the woods where the trail gets more interesting taking you over roots and undulating woody terrain. The trail has a distinctly French feel to it, as here you are deep in the heart of the French countryside and woodlands.

10 Track Junction

Head right again at the junction of trails to work your way back around the hill with a wooden sign post to Chapelle de Jacquicourt. As you lose height here, look for a gap in the trees for a brief view of le Griffre Torrent to your left.

11 Veruy

Go right staying on this track at the next fork with a smaller track. At the next fork, go right again almost back on yourself, then turning round to the left as the slope turns down more steeply and speeds you up. When the track hits a tarmac road, turn on to it and follow it for a short distance, turning off to the right to run along side the road for a brief time.

12 Electric Fence / Pole

Go through the electric pole gate to a VTT marker No.6 and at the right hand bend ahead, drop down to your left following VTT6 to a rough rocky and muddy down slope.

13 Downhill

At the next couple of main trail junctions keep heading down the hill taking a right then a quick left.

14 Road Head

This hits the main tarmac road at the south end of Les Gets.

15 Right Turn

Head right for a slow steady uphill bearing to the left to bring you back to the centre town.

Getting There

Take t he Mont Chery lift from the main road in Les Gets. Exit the lift and roll rightwards down to a small chair lift. As you go up on this you pass the Kona Bike Park, with its impressive ramps and jumps, on the ridge line on the right. Then you go over the start of the Mont Chéry / Les Gets 2 DH, as it traverses across the field to your left.

Start Points

At the top of the chair lift, exit right, and continue straight down to the Bike Park c take a quick left under the chairlift cables to get on to the Mont Chéry DH.

Kona Bike Park

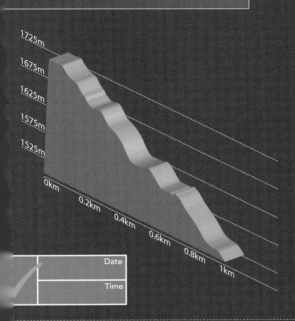

1725m
1675m
1625m
1575m
1525m

0km
0.2km
0.4km
0.6km
0.8km
1km

	Date
	Time

Mont Chéry

DH

Whatever grade
you want to
make it!

5

500 m

Often

Many Lifetimes

IGN 3528
Morzine

Mont Chéry/Les Gets 2

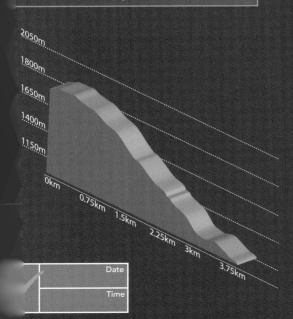

2050m
1800m
1650m
1400m
1150m

0km
0.75km
1.5km
2.25km
3km
3.75km

	Date
	Time

Mont Chéry

Downhill

DH

Hard

3

2.75 km

580 m

7 - 20 mins

IGN 3528
Morzine

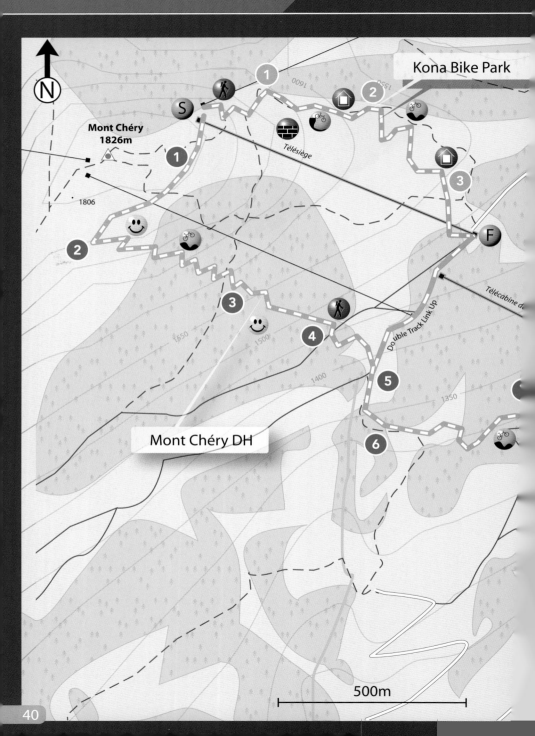

Kona Bike Park

Mont Chéry
1826m

Mont Chéry DH

500m

les Gets

DH Summary: Kona Bike Park

The Kona Bike Park is a reasonably sizeable area crammed with an assortment of jumps, drops, berms and wall rides. Some of the lines are a bit on the tight side and take a bit of getting used to. However when you do get used to them there is a lot of fun to be had. There are so many different obstacles and lines that it would take a long time to get bored if you enjoy this type of thing.

With many of the bigger jumps coming off the ridge line, the area has also got some of the most photographic spots in the whole region.

DH Summary: Mont Chéry DH

The Mont Chéry or "Les Gets 2" downhill is a typical DH track including berms, jumps and wooded sections. The track includes everything you could want from a downhill course apart from a technical rock section - but some people will be glad of that! The track is situated on the same slope that has been used for many a World Cup and even the World Championships in 2004. The track starts with a long off camber grass section into various tight corners. Then through some very rooty trees, a short roller coaster section before the trail starts to open up. And this trail isn't finished 'till the fat lady sings'. The very last section is an exceedingly fast steep bermed field where you'll always see plenty of people psyching themselves up for the finish.

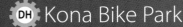 Kona Bike Park

Before you get to the park itself, you have to make it down through a long series of tight bermed corners. These are very good practise for getting your cornering dialled. If at first you are not keen, its worth persevering as this section does become more fun the more you get used to it.

1 Drop offs

Arriving at a small fence you are at the top of the park and have three options. The left option is off a medium sized drop onto a steep landing, the middle option is a large drop off a wooden hut onto the same landing. The right hand option is the most simple and is just a series of tight corners.

2 Hip jump

After doing either of the drops you are then faced with a large hip jump. Again three options - off either side or straight down the middle and drop off the end and turn left to meet up with the left hand hip.

Each variation has other variations again. It would take this whole book to explain them all. It's best you just go and look for yourself. As with ridding anywhere, always check what you're about to go over!

3 Singletrack

When you reach the bottom of the park, there is a wooden hut to the far left, the exit of the park is just below and to the right.

Continue down the hill along some fast enjoyable single-track to the fire-road at the bottom.

You can now either go back up for another go (turn left to get back on the lift) or, turn right and follow the fire-road for a couple hundred metres and you meet up with the bottom half of the Les Gets 2 / Mont Chéry Downhill.

Mont Chéry

1 Grassy bumps

The track starts with a fairly slow grassy section with some large bumps and tight corners. Then there is a long straight off camber grass section before more tight corners and off camber dirt section through a couple of trees. This then joins in with the old track.

2 Berms and roots

Just a short right then left berm before your first taste of roots. Coming into the trees you have three lines, right then through to left is the smoothest. Small slope into tight right-hander is hard to get right first time but after a couple of runs you get used to it.

3 Look out for the trees!

Into the tree section, again there are plenty of lines to choose from, here it's more personal preference. When you get to the wide, slightly off camber, straight, beware of the tricky left-hander at the bottom. Try to keep it ion the rut and when round the corner try to get the high line. Flattish section, tight right, tighter switchback and the next fire road.

4 Pre-jump

Drop in off the fire road, take the left-hander and there is a nice little step-down, a slight right bend and pre-jump the next slope. This is worth checking out first before riding as it can be quite tight if riding with much speed. From the bottom of the small slope there is a small left before a quite hard floaty couple of right-handers. A left hand berm and another

tight switchback and across another fire road.

5 Roller coaster

Here you have a collection of small corners and jumps before a couple of trees and roots mark the start of a great roller-coaster section which is fun at a medium pace and hard when going full on. Beware on the next small slope as the following corners are quite tight and usually blown out.

6 Table top

The track opens up for a fast left right left with a berm on the first. Tight right, slight sweep left and right, then keep it low until just before the next corner. Swing up high and drop down into the tight left-hander, berm right then left. Over a couple of deceptive jumps, keep it low over the second to make it round the right-hander. Straightaway turn left over some fairly large roots and drop down through a couple of quick left right berms. Over the tabletop, through a fast left right left and over some small rollers.

7 Exposed and steep!

If you're tired at this point it may be worth getting a couple of breaths as the next field section is quite full on. First you have a few easy corners before traversing the open field and through a couple of trees. Start concentrating now as it starts to get steep. You then have a series of similar bermed corners, but no more steep shoots. It gets a bit steeper when approaching the trees towards the bottom; two more flat corners and you're at the road.

bikefax

Mont Chéry to Morzine

Les Gets

Summary

For many riders, arriving in the Morzine area for the first time is a daunting business, wondering where to go and what to do first. For this reason countless mountain bikers end up on the gentler slopes of Les Gets first. As an opening ride this trail, linking Mont Chéry to Morzine, gives you the opportunity to stretch the legs, trial some of the downhill sections at Les Gets and figure out how the whole area links together.

That's not to say though that this route is a 'pussy cat'. The riding is typical of the area, with lots of wiggling around through the trees, and steep earthy descents to prepare your head for some of the fiercer riding at Morzine itself. However doing it away from the main slopes first means you've got time to slow it down if you need to and to get your head for the steeps back in shape.

Mont Chéry

Expert

Hard

18km

510m

1300m

2-3 hrs

IGN 3258 ET Morzine

At the end of the ride you are well placed to either head into Morzine and up the Téléphérique de Plenay ready to sample the 'Avalanche Cup' Downhill Course, or amble back up to Les Gets, back up to Mont Chéry and section together the rest of the Les Gets Downhill.

Getting There

Mont Chéry is on the north side of the Les Gets Valley and the lift station is just near the roundabout at the north east end of the town on the road heading off to Morzine.

If you're coming from the Morzine direction, the lift is on your right just as you enter town. There is plenty of parking on the right behind the lift station or just after the roundabout on the left.

Start Point

Take the Télécabine du Mont Chéry to the half way station. From here head out of the lift and go leftwards to the Télésiège de la Grande Ours chairlift and take this to the top of the hill.

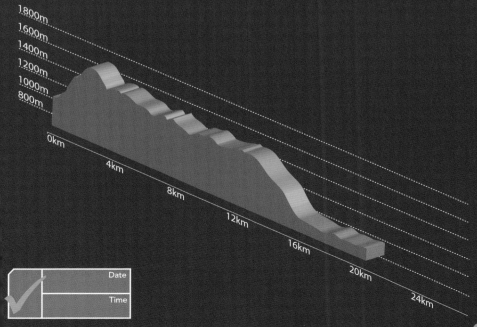

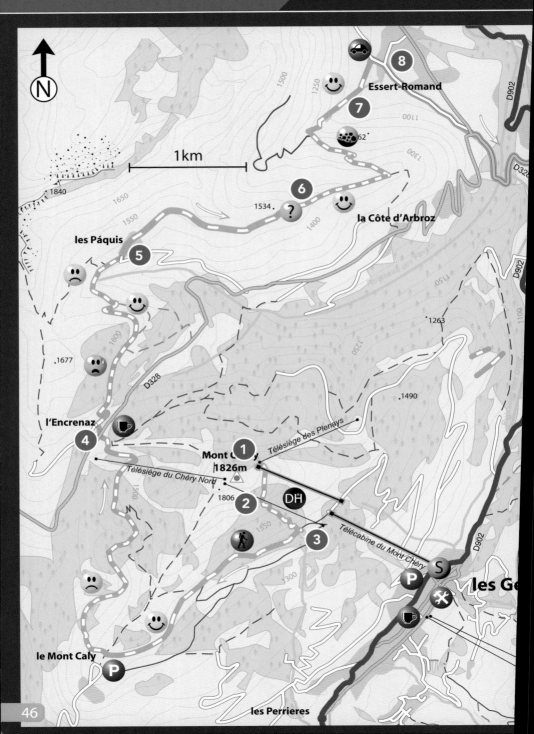

N

1km

1840

Essert-Romand

1500
1250
1100
1300

62

1534

6

?

la Côte d'Arbroz

les Páquis

5

1650
1550
1400

1150

1263

1600

1677

.1490

l'Encrenaz

D328

1750

4

1

Mont Chéry
1826m

Télésiège des Plenays

1806

2

DH

Télésiège du Chéry Nord

1500

1550

3

Télécabine du Mont Chéry

S

P

les Ge

1300

le Mont Caly

P

les Perrieres

D902
D328
D902
D902

Montriond

Morzine

les Chavannes

Mont Chery to Morzine

(1) Top of Télésiège de la Grande Ours

When you step off the chair lift head down rightwards and on the first bend just after the lift, go right at the fork. Go under the chairlift and traverse across the field. Stay high at a faint fork and then drop down to join the big track and down hill course.

(2) Downhill Course

Join the Downhill Course at a wide track on a sweeping bend. Straightaway this narrows to a rutted double track and then descends steeply to take a narrow rooted and earthy line through the trees.

Drop off this on to a section of double track with the occasional electric fence barrier on it. If you see these barriers covered in yellow and black plastic tape you can ride straight through them. Otherwise take care it would be pretty nasty to hit one that didn't open at speed. At the end of this section of the DH course the trail crosses a wide forest road. Stop here.

(3) Forest Track

Turn right and continue along this wide track all the way to the village of Encrenaz. The trail starts as a fast wide track, then turning into undulating singletrack just after passing the village of Mont Caly. Eventually it widens out once again as it emPties you out in the village of Encrenaz.

4 Encrenaz

There are plenty of nice little bars and restaurants in Encrenaz as well as a water fountain for a top up. But if its too early in the day to stop, carry straight on and up the hill by the sign posts. Go steeply up the tarmac briefly and then fork off right on a wide stony track. Unfortunately there is a brutal bit of climbing just at the start here.

Fear not for the climbing is finally rewarded with a very long flowing section of downhill on fast grassy doubletrack. A bit of re-ascent takes you up a signposted junction at Les Paquis.

5 Les Paquis

Go straight on at the junction and follow a track to just after Pt 1534m, and what appears to be the end of the trail.

6 Track End

Going straight on in front of you is the start of some fun steep singletrack. The view of the valley ahead is spectacular, with the tiny villages dwarfed by the surrounding mountains, reminding you of just how much descent there is yet to go. Initially, the trail is straight and narrow as it plunges through a grassy opening in the forest, after which it heads darkly into the woods and becomes more technical, with roots and stumps galore.

7 Small Path Junction

Deep in the trees (just after a very steep root section) you arrive at a small path junction. Follow the VTT sign and head off to the left. The narrow earthy trail continues wiggling on down through the trees eventually widening out and changing its character into a stony loose track.

8 Loose Stony Track

The stony track continues steeply down through the trees to a fork. Go right at the fork and continue with more of the same bone shaking speedy descending.

9 Minor Road

At the bottom of the stony track you come out onto a small road. Turn right and go along until you join onto the D329. Turn right on the main road and climb for a while to a T junction with the D902. At a roundabout, turn left to go into Morzine or right to return to Les Gets.

bikefax

Tour du Mont Chéry

Les Gets

Summary

Quickly get off the beaten track at Mont Chéry, lunch at the beautiful village of Encrenaz, and then blast back into Les Gets for more exploring. Alternatively race around the trail and then fully warmed up, follow up with a fun afternoon of downhill action on Mont Chéry pistes.

Starting off as broad fire road, the trail gives you a chance to warm up the legs before a little light ascending on wide singletrack. Undulating paths then take you down into the village of Encrenaz where if you've timed it right, lunch beckons.

From here double back on yourself slightly and head into the woods on the north side of the mountain and after a short bit of climbing pick up trails heading swiftly downhill and back into Les Gets.

Mont Chéry Lift	
Classic	
Hard	
13 km	
175 m	
450 m	
1 .5 hrs	
IGN 3528 Morzine	

With nothing too technical or taxing, this is a route suited to all kinds of riders, from those wanting an hour or so away from the crowds to those new to the sport.

Getting There

At the Morzine end of Les Gets, take the Télésiège du Mont Chéry upwards. Exit the lift at the mid station and ride leftwards towards the La Pointe chairlift.

Start Point

From the bottom of the La Pointe chairlift follow the VTT signs leftwards going under the chair lift and up the track passing the DH course as it crosses the fire road.

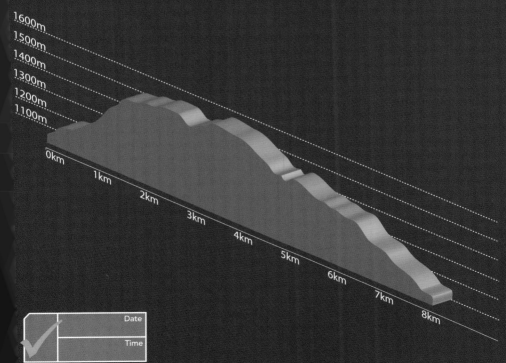

N

1840

Essert-Romand

1162

1534

la Côte d'Arbroz

les Pâquis

Le Plancouard 5

.1263

1337. Lassare

4 P

.1490

6

Encrenaz

P

2 Télésiège du Chéry Nord

Télésiège des Plenays

Mont Chéry
1826m

1806

Télécabine du Mont Chéry

1

F

S

les Gets

P

le Mont Caly

P

1km

le Perrieres

Tour du Mont Chéry

1 Fire Road

The trail starts as a fast wide track, then turns into undulating singletrack, afterwards widening out once again as it takes you towards the village of Encrenaz.

There are fantastic views as you head towards the first village of Mont Caly. Don't turn down here, instead carry on around the mountainside, but keep at least one eye on the track, as this section is also popular with walkers.

2 Encrenaz

Just before the village of Encrenaz go right and re-ascend steeply, but briefly. Again the trail undulates pleasantly until you to come to a section that was washed out by an avalanche.

The trail has been rebuilt and now gives some short sharp descents and some even sharper re-ascents. Once past here the trail continues on through the trees eventually turning into a wide forest track.

3 Chairlift Cables

Follow the forest track, feeling like you are suddenly in the middle of nowhere, until you see some lift cables above you. Just after going under the cables (ignore the TT signposted) turn off going steeply off to the right - you can go up here if you want. It takes you straight back to the Mont Chéry lift station, but be warned even though it's the official way back - it's a brutal ascent.

4 Lassare Parking area

At the road take the singletrack heading back to the NE towards Le Plancouard. The trail goes steeply down the hillside making its way in and out of the trees to eventually join up with another small road at Le Plancouard.

5 Le Plancouard

Turn right and follow the rough track back as it traverses more steadily around the hillside following the Ruisseau des Gets (stream) back towards Les Gets.

6 Les Nantes

At a collection of buildings at Les Nantes join a back road which takes you up to the main Morzine to Les Gets road, turning right to get back to the lift station.

Col de Coux

Les Gets

Summary

This ride uses some of the longest and fastest lifts in the area to allow you to cover some amazing ground and ride some stunning singletrack, all in superb scenery.

The lift access joins together both both singletrack and fast stone track descents, with one super-tough climb thrown in as well. For the cross country purists out there, all of the lifts can be by-passed and additional climbs done instead - good luck!

On route you visit three of the main downhill bike parks in the area, and if you've still got energy to spare, you can include laps on some of these courses too!

The last climb up to the Col de Coux is a challenging one but this is more than rewarded by the fantastic singletrack to be found elsewhere on the route. Just get in gear and enjoy!

Les Gets	
Expert	
Extreme	
32 km	
270 m	
1830 m	
4 -6 hrs	
IGN 3528 Morzine	

Start Point

Start in Les Gets by the Mont Chéry lift station. There's plenty of parking behind the station or just up the road as you head into town.

The advantage of starting in Les Get is that you finish off at exactly the same place that you started, with the 4X course at Les Chavannes as a fitting finale to the ride.

Alternatively - Start in Morzine at the Super Morzine lift, and ride from Les Gets back to Morzine at the end of the day.

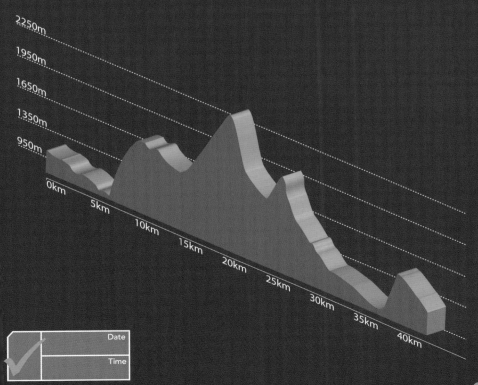

Morzine

1554

les Gets

D902

2250m

1950m

1650m

1350m

950m

0km 5km 10km 15km 20km 25km 30km 35km 40km

Date

Time

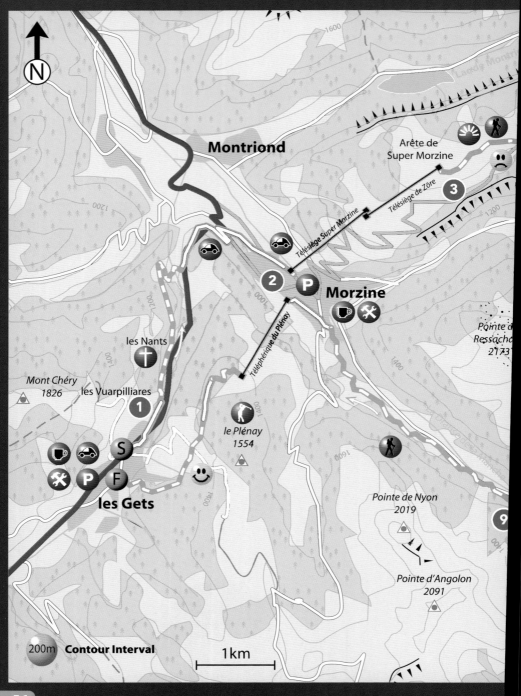

N

Montriond

Arête de
Super Morzine

Téléski de Zöre

3

Télésiège Super Morzine

2

P

Morzine

Pointe d
Ressacho
2173

Téléphérique du Plénay

les Nants

Mont Chéry
1826

les Vuarpilliares

1

le Plénay
1554

S

P   F

les Gets

Pointe de Nyon
2019

9

Pointe d'Angolon
2091

200m   **Contour Interval**

1km

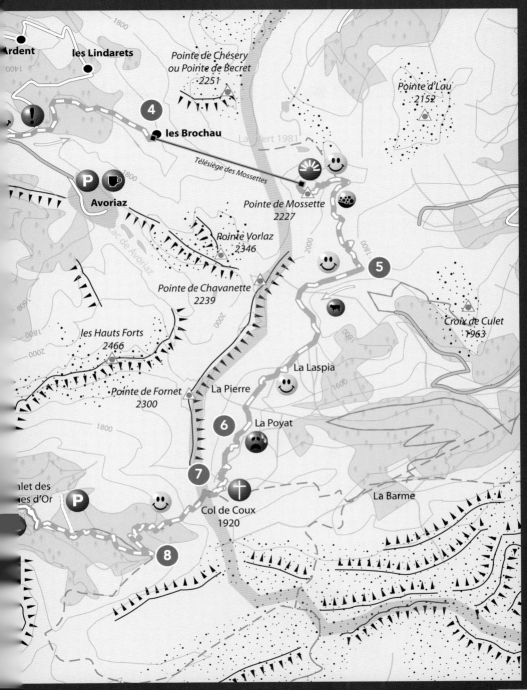

Ardent
les Lindarets
Pointe de Chésery
ou Pointe de Becret
2251
Pointe d'Lau
2152

4

les Brochau

Avoriaz

Télésiège des Mossettes

Pointe de Mossette
2227

Pointe Vorlaz
2346

Pointe de Chavanette
2239

5

Croix de Culet
1963

les Hauts Forts
2466

La Laspia

Pointe de Fornet
2300

La Pierre

6 La Poyat

7

La Barme

alet des
es d'Or

P

Col de Coux
1920

8

Route Description

① Les Gets

Head out of Les Gets towards Morzine, following the main road but then taking the back road off to the left atPt1136m - Les Vuarpillieres. Follow the back road along past Les Nants and onto some smooth rolling off-road single and double track running down to le Plancouard. Follow the road up past the chapel and back onto the main road, heading down into Morzine and to the base of the Super Morzine lift.

② Lift Stations

Take the Super Morzine lift up and then the de Zore lift, up to the top of the Super Morzine arête.

③ Super Morzine Arête

At the top of the lift turn right and follow the footpath along the top of the arête until you reach the road atPt1760m - Col de la Joux Verte.

There are various signs along here directing bikes one way and walkers another. Right next to the t-junction at the col is a singletrack route, labelled as a red cycling route, heading off to the NE. Follow this for a really enjoyable descending and contouring piece of singletrack, as it crosses the path of the old French national downhill (amazing route!) and passes to the right of the reservoir to finally reach the base of the Mossettes lift.

④ Mossettes Lift

Take the Mossettes lift up. From the top of the lift follow the main, wide stony track down southwards, taking the first left turn after a short distance, heading now further into Switzerland. Follow this track down, past a major junction where the track splits - head right here - and go down a short distance to where there is a smaller singletrack going off to the right. (GR 3322 51177). There is a no cycling sign here (!) so follow the singletrack off to the right for some good technical riding. Contour along past the alpine cows until you reach another wide rough stone track just above Chaux Palin at Pt. 1844m.

⑤ Les Creuses Traverse

Follow the track along southwards, passing Le lapisa, La Pierre and La Poyat, turning right at the junction just after La Poyat. A fast wide stony track.

⑥ Plane de Coux Climb

Turn right at this small junction and get into your granny gear, climbing up the steep and wide stony track, around switchback after switchback. This 270m climb is steady, but watch out for the steep bits on the corner of every switchback!! Pass through one gate but keep on heading upwards. Reach the Col de Coux and take a deserved break, looking at the amazing views!

⑦ GR5 Descent

Head through the gate back into France and enjoy the astounding singletrack descent or the GR5. Good technical riding, never too steep, with amazing views as you go. The track changes between tight singletrack and slightly wider stone track as you head down. Follow the track down until you reach the wide stone track just next to the Torrent de Chardonniere.

8 Track and Road descent

Follow the track down to the turning for the Chalet des Mines d'Or, and then continue down on the road into l'Erigne derriere. Watch out for the singletrack heading off across an open field to the left here, signed as a red VTT route. Take this track.

9 La Dranse stone track

Follow the wide stone track running alongside la Dranse until it spits you out onto the road at the SE end of Morzine. Turn left and climb up the hill and follow the road along to get to the Plenay lift and into town for a refreshment stop.

You can either finish here, or take the Plenay lift up, heading down and across back into Les Gets past the top of the Tennis Courts run, or ride along the Plenay ridge and back to the top of the Chavannes lift, and then down into Les Gets.

D902

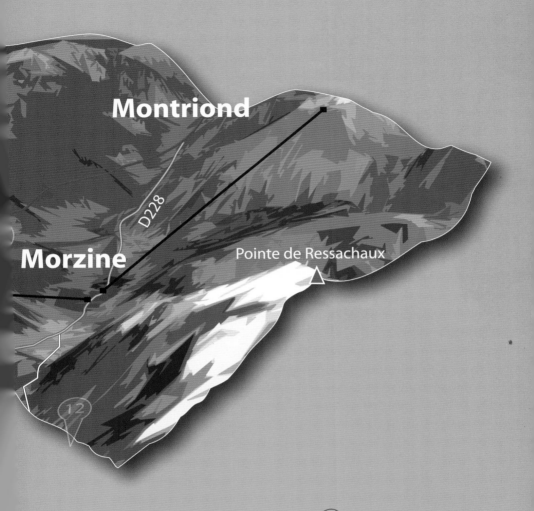

Montriond

D228

Morzine

Pointe de Ressachaux

Introduction

Starting from the centre of Morzine, the Plenay and the Super Morzine lifts give effortless access to sign posted routes for all abilities. Le Plenay's permanent downhill track has already seduced a large number of professional mountain bikers: from the French and International riders of the Avalanche Cup to the Free Raid Classic mountain bike magazine readers. This activity is no way reserved for elite class athletes as a mountain bike ride in this environment can easily end up as an afternoon nap in the middle of an alpine meadow.

For Cross Country riders, you have a choice of putting yourself through lung-busting climbs or taking one of the two lifts out of the town on either side of the valley, both of which will transport up to the top of the ridges. Either way you'll be sure to get fantastic views, great singletrack and massive descents.

For the DH lovers, Morzine is held in high esteem with some of the longest, the most established and the best maintained DH specific trails in the area.

Getting there

Follow directions for getting to Les Gets and then continue just another couple of miles further north along the road to arrive in Morzine.

Activities / shops etc

Morzine is a hub of entertainment and host to many activities including paragliding, horse riding, canyoning and climbing as well as mountain biking. You won't be disappointed with the atmosphere in this lively alpine town.

If you want more than just mountain biking there is a Luge run just to the right of the Plenay lift descending 150m, plus a small Bungee Jump at the Telepherique de Nyon (80m in height). You can also find an Indiana Park here too where you can scale the heights of apparatus up in the trees. Through the Tourist Information Centre you can find many activities which are guided such as the Cascade Adventure where you can get wet through abseiling down waterfalls and jumping into plunge pools for a change from standing on your pedals.

Bike shops & hire

The road running directly down the hill into Morzine centre from the Plenay lift station is continually becoming more bike orientated with Caribou Sports offering VTT hire, bike wash, repairs and air pump and various sports clothing shops line this road. Taking a right turn and following the high street down to the south end of town quickly brings you to a great selection of shops including 'Twinner' with a 'Technician du Sport' to help fix you bike plus a small stock of equipment and clothing. If you go left down the high street by the café and continue on for 100m, you will come to

MistyFly; a cool little shop containing more and more biking-wear goggles and sunnys. Bike hire is generally available from local activity providers and shops from 15 euros for a half day or 25 euros for a whole day.

Food

With a very busy winter season in Morzine, a multitude of eating places has sprung up, from the road-side cafes to very high quality restaurants. For a quick snack there are several small outdoor cafes in Morzine including the very convenient 'Burger Place' opposite the bottom of the Plenay lift.

There's also a great outdoor café called La Main a La Pate on the other side of the road from 'Twinner' where you can get a value lunch from a smiling face and sit outside with your bike. A few metres away from the bottom of the Super Morzine lift is a really great little café in a wooden hut called L'Ancor. L'ancor serves fantastic chocolate crepes, and you can sit outside with your bike or get a snack for the lift journey.

The Dixie Bar, (on the lower main street through the town centre heading toward Les Gets) run by British owners and French staff, is a great place to get lunch and sit outside between DH or XC runs. Ther village has plenty of other bars and restaurants based in hotels and as separate venues, as well as a couple of night clubs, one of which, the 'Opera', sporadically puts on foam parties like those of Ibiza!

Accommodation

The majority of accommodation in Morzine is in the form of both traditional and modern wooden chalets. Booking in advance is a must especially during July and August. The tourist season carries on just a bit longer in Morzine than in Les Gets and other smaller towns, so it's a good place for a late summer break. However, Morzine closes down its services and lifts by mid September so don't leave it too late.

Some great places to stay include : The Ridge Hotel at the Montriond side of Morzine. The hotel looks back over the town centre and with a great atmosphere and bar, plus a weekly barbeque is a comfortable and friendly place to stay.

Alpine Tracks, Mountain Bike Holidays and Challenge Activ are all great to if you are looking for an inclusive deal with bike hire, storage and repairs available.

Also have a look at Morzinelets.com for accommodation as they provide a free shuttle service tel:+ 0450790750. For those wanting a little more comfort, The Grand Hotel near the centre of town has a huge number of rooms and excellent service.

Many hotels have connections with or own chalets, so be sure to ask what is available, in order to gain the full choice before making a decision on where to stay.

Useful contacts

Misty Fly Bike shop for ride information
Tourist information centre +33 (0)450747272.
Montriond Tourist Office +33(0)450791281
Maison de la Montagne +33 450759665
Ecole de VTT Synergie +33 687390014

Restaurant Le Clin d'Ceil +33 450790310
www.montriond-portesdusoleil.com
www.bikemorzine.com
www.alpinetracks.co.uk
www.morzine-avoriaz.com
www.morzinelets.com
www.theridgehotel.com
www.mountainbikeholidays.co.uk
www.challenge-activ.com

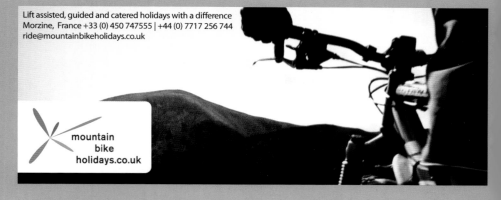

Lift assisted, guided and catered holidays with a difference
Morzine, France +33 (0) 450 747555 | +44 (0) 7717 256 744
ride@mountainbikeholidays.co.uk

mountain
bike
holidays.co.uk

Summer adventures with Alpine Tracks

Alpine Tracks have spent many hours in the saddle and on foot developing an exciting programme of mountain biking, walking and climbing in Europe. Featured here are just two of the great summer adventures Alpine Tracks have to offer this summer.

Morzine
Mountain Bike 'Must Do'

Morzine is considered as one of 'the places' to mountain bike in the Alps. The area is superb with hundreds of miles of tracks and paths to explore as well as 7 purpose-built downhill courses, all serviced by a network of cable cars and chairlifts. We have put together a cross country week with some big climbs, awesome single track, huge descents coupled with stunning scenery. Minibus and chairlift support. 6 nights in Morzine, 1 night in mountain refuge.

Chalet Eira - your luxury Morzine accommodation

Morzine not only offers great mountain bike adventures, but also other exciting activities, including white water rafting and horse riding.

Accommodation is in Chalet Eira based on twin share of an ensuite room inc breakfast and afternoon tea. The chalet has its own bike shop run by Mud Sweat Gears, large bar, lounge, restaurant, sauna and jacuzzi. One night is spent in a mountain refuge.

Portes du Soleil 'Free Ride paradise'

Getting there is easy. Flights are available from London Heathrow, Gatwick, Luton, Manchester, Edinburgh and Dublin with Swiss, British Airways and Easy Jet. The transfer to Morzine takes roughly 1 hour by comfortable minibuses. If you bring your own bike, we do have a custom-built mountain bike trailer.

Morzine is a comfortable 8 hour drive from Calais. We can book your Channel crossing on either the ferry or via Euro Tunnel. We also provide a detailed route map and directions to Morzine.

Norway
Fabulous fjord country

For something really different consider a stunning 7 day guided and supported mountain bike adventure through the heartland of Norway taking in the Navvies road to the spectacular Fjord country, finishing off with lift assisted riding around the ski resort of Voss. The trip is relatively strenuous with 1 night spent in a catered mountain hotel.

"Awesome day, woke up with the sun glinting off the glacier, huge Norwegian breakfast, gentle climb to get the legs going, then we had a 1500m descent over 45kms right down to the fjord at Flam. Beers and swims just magic - many thanks"

Neil Newman - 9 September, 2004

Wonderful Norwegian scenery

Ride through the heartland of Norway

We have built in one free day which we plan to take during the later part of the trip – though this may vary depending upon weather conditions at the time. The holiday is made up of 3 differing mountain biking mini adventures!

Our tours meet at Oslo Airport, transfers to Geilo and from Voss are by rail. Flights to Oslo are available with both SAS and British Airways.

If you would like to include this tour within an extended holiday in Norway please contact us to discuss meeting points other than Oslo. Similarly if you wish to travel with one of the low cost carriers eg Ryan Air or Norwegian.no or even by cruise ferry from Newcastle to Bergen then please contact us and we can suggest alternative meeting points.

Alpine Tracks full summer programme features:

- Morzine - Mountain Biking, White Water Rafting, Horse Riding, And much more...
- Freeriding Les 2 Alpes
- Norway - MTB Epic
- Mont Blanc - Climbing

Be adventurous - Give Alpine Tracks a call!

Freephone 0800 0282546

Check out our Website! www.alpinetracks.com

Getting There

Head into the centre of Morzine and turn up to the sign posted Télésiège de Plenay. You will turn right to the lift if coming from Les Gets and left if coming in from the opposite direction. Season, week or day passes can be bought at the booking office. Take a ride up the hill in one of the most comfortable télésiège the area has and step out into the cooler air. If not, look right to a tall VTT sign post for 'VTT Permanent' and on to a small wooden hut to start the course.

Start Points

Looking down the hill when you come out of the lift is a wide path heading straigh down the hill then veering off left. At the top of this is usually a time trial start gate Either head down through the field and onto the wide path or through the start gate

‍alanche Cup

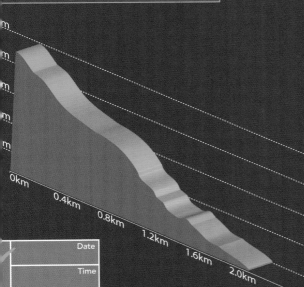

	Date
	Time

Télécabine du Plenay

Downhill DH

Extreme ④

3.5km

550m

5-45m

IGN Morzine 3528

‍alanche Cup Variation

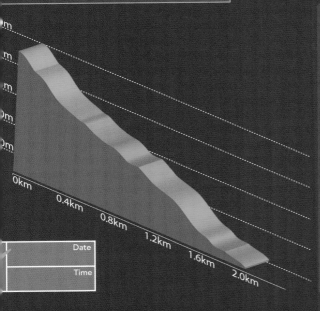

	Date
	Time

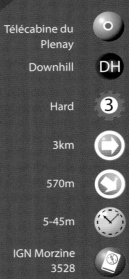

Télécabine du Plenay

Downhill DH

Hard ③

3km

570m

5-45m

IGN Morzine 3528

N

le Plan Morand

la Crusaz

F
P

Avalanche Cup

Avalanche Cup Var.

Téléphérique du Plenar y

Télésiege d'Attray

1247

1350

1450

1250

500m

DH Avalanche Cup

DH Variation

The Avalanche Cup is a smooth, flowing and long course, that descends the Plenay from top to bottom. To ride this course in one hit is physically demanding but great fun and sectioning it a few times to get the best lines can be just as much fun. Full body armour is a must on this track as there are tight turns, steep rutted slopes and some fast jumps (if you're that way inclined).

There are some sections where you'll find track variations to choose from if you're not flying past too fast. Some can stretch your capability and add interest; some are just a bit easier and/or faster so use your head before bombing straight down them.

This variation on the popular Avalanche Cup trail is less busy and makes a good option for a mixed group of both DH and XC riders. The trail is characterised by sweeping open descents and not too much technical bike work.

Great for a quick blast and a good outing for cross country riders wanting to push the pace on a bit. It's a fast ride throughout, but be cautious as it shares the mid part of the route with walkers - one to keep your eyes open on.

(DH) Avalanche Cup

(1) Wooden hut start

Roll down into the hut with a racing feeling then straight out the other side. Look out for a drainage gully and then let gravity take you down around some easy bends. A flat gravely section past a hut to the left then takes you into a fast left hand turn through some trees where you'll pick up speed into the open. Keep a racing line as the trail flows down then back up a smooth steep straight to bring you back into the woods.

Next, look out for a steep rutted area that takes you into a tight left hand bend and down a steep slope back into the field.

(2) Berms and jumps

Sweep around the high off-camber right hand bend in the field, stay close to the right, then level up for a quick jump on a small straight. Take a 90 degree left turn at a junction and stay left for a high right hand berm taking you straight back into the woods. Building up speed through several small jumps and a fast rooty section, ride down into a rutted slope until it turns upward for a quick jump into the open.

(3) Styling it!

Speed across a fire-road to a small double jump with a long down slope landing through an open field. This is a good place for styling it up if you have the skills and, if you're lucky, the local sports photographer will be there to catch you in action. (Any bike-friendly shop in Morzine will tell you where to find him to purchase a copy for a small fee).

[Alternative to 2. Instead of taking a 90-degree turn left, go straight on into the woods. Beware very rooty and rutted. Interesting alternative and well worthy of a look, but is rough and rarely gets maintained and includes a jump, but care is to be taken when re-joining the main track.]

(4) Switch backs

Sweep around several fun fast switchbacks taking a racing line and catch your breath ready for the next technical section. Flowing back into the woods for a quick left hand turn, check your speed as you head down a bank into an off-camber rocky straight. Here you have 3 choices:

1   Go straight on through the trees down a very steep section.

2   Take a very slight right turn into a very steep long left hand berm known as 'the ten percent'.

3   Take a full right turn down a rocky section of fast fire road sweeping back round to the left.

(5) Concrete tunnel

The tree alternatives now all join up for a quick straight with an optional jump to the right bringing you to a rooty section with more small jumps dropping you down into the woods. Cross an old fire-road at speed to a small jump into a not too high left hand turn that shoots you through a concrete tunnel

DH Variation

1 Track Junction

At the junction of routes with the sharp 90 degree turn left taking you down the permanent Avalanche Cup track, instead turn 90 degree right and head down the open grassy slope between two small woods.

[At this junction, there is the start of yet another trail variation which you can follow if you go straight on into the lower woods section. This is steep and technical].

As you fly down the grassy slope, look out for and hop the ever present drainage gullies to an electric fence. Don't panic, as with care at speed you can hop over the metal bar roll-over in the fence gap and just keep going. Check out the fantastic views if you're not at top speed here.

2 Fast Section

Picking up good speed here, look out, as you can easily be fed into the narrow water worn gullies in the track as you come up to the bottom of the piste. Careful, cos if you get stuck in them, you'll be thrown you off line for the fence gap and the metal bar step at the bottom.

3 Fence Gap

After this gap you come right out on to a multi-use track and head down to a small group of wooden buildings to the right. Take the sign posted 'VTT difficile' left turn just before the buildings.

Watch out for pedestrians, as you briefly drop down to another poorly maintained fire road which turns back to the left. After only 50m take the right turn on to singletrack running parallel with the fire road and follow this briefly until you turns back right on yourself and scoot up into the woods on a quick rise.

4 Roots & Switchbacks

After a brief section tackling roots and fast turns, quickly tackle some fast switchbacks and pop back out of the woods for a very fast tight left turn to join on to another piece of singletrack. Look out for pedestrians here.

5 Final Blast

Follow the track skirting along the bottom of the woods and across the field back to the lift station.

NB: if the bottom field trail is under maintenance a detour may be signed taking you down across the field slightly sooner than the regular trail taking you to the small lift car park.

Avalanche Cup

Take this turn too high and you'll miss this entrance!

Pop out of the tunnel to a down slope followed by a fast straight section with some bumpy sweeping turns and exposed roots. Enjoy the shade for a moment before you pop out by 'Poste 15' at a fork in the track.

6 Poste 15

At 'Post 15' in the woods you have 2 choices:

1 'Difficile/ Beginner'. Go left for a less technical but very fast straight over a wooden path that turns quickly right at the end to re-join the main track.

OR

2 Go straight on, for a steep rutted high right hand bend where you need to stay right and sweep around some tight bends bringing you back round to the left to a technical jump section. Avoid this by staying right .

7 Big jump

After a couple more turns come out of the trees checking your speed to a built up potentially big jump into right hand down slope.

Stay tight right to avoid this. Keep your speed for a steep up slope jumping into the woods and making the most of a couple of drops before deep (often muddy) switchbacks. Take a central line leaving a fast left turn down to a double jump or stay left out of the turn to avoid this.

A tight right hand bend comes up immediately after it. Follow the track down a left hand gully berm flowing into some tight bends and short, technical rooty section. Stay aware for a tight left then right-hander, with steep drop to the right bringing you out on to the bottom rocky fire road.

8 Taped section alongside fire road

Follow along the tape marked straight, giving the huge right hand wall ride a go and go on past the bike wash hut.

The very last part of the track then takes a couple of fast sweeping turns on silky ground across the field. Try to avoid the temptation to jump the wooden bridge over the Devalkart and you're back at the lifts.

Get more from Morzine

with Morzinelets.com the specialist biking company in Morzine

e & Protection Hire

n only £12.99 per week

ed in December 2005
e winter season,
Sports are proud
fer the best kit
ble. We offer
hire, servicing
riendly advice
our team of
ed staff.

Bikes - from £25 per day
ngoose Bikes - from £20 per day
dy & head Protection from £3 per day

Qualified local guides

From only £20 per day!

Take a freeride tour of The Portes du Soleil with one of local guides. Our guides are all riders from the local area and know all the secret spots. They will be able to show you the best cross country, downhill and free riding in one of the best domains in the world for mountain biking.

All our guides are french registered and have all the relevant certificates and insurance to make sure you are in the best hands.

Our guides aim is to take you somewhere you might not have found without local knowledge. You don't have to look at the map, he will know the area inside out, where to stop for lunch, where the good views are and where the next water stop is..

Local Accommodation

From only £38 per person per night

For the best choice of quality hotels budget hotels and apartments in Morzine.

- The Ridge Half board Hotels - from £50pn
- The Rhodos B&B Hotel - from only £35pn
- L'Olympique Penthouse - From £80pw
- La Vallee Verte - From £50pw

t our website **www.morzinelets.com** to get more from Morzine

Amazing downhill tracks

crazy

100's of natural jump

The perfect holiday!!

World Class Downhilling

You don't have to be a seasoned mountain bike rider to enjoy all the 650 km of trails tracks that Morzine and the Portes Du Soleil have to offer . There are plenty of easy-cruising beginner trails that offer fun, excitement and alpine views unlike any you've seen before.

There are ten permanent downhill pistes in the Portes du Soleil. With one lift pass you can ride the celebrated tracks on Mont Chery (Coup du monde 2004) the "north shore" in Morgins and many other hidden freeride spots if you ask the local riders. All the downhill tracks are graded by colour black runs being the most difficult.

At Morzinelets we can provide you with a professional guiding service, bike and protection hire.
If you're really passionate about your riding and want to experience some of the best singletrack, freeride and downhill tracks in the world this is the PLACE to come

FIND OUT MORE AT
www.morzinelets.com

Arête du Berroi

Morzine

Summary

The Arete de Berroi ride includes some pretty tough climbs that are however rewarded by access to some of the most wonderful, flowing singletrack descents in the area.

Combine this route with as many descents of the numerous downhill courses that you encounter on this route, and you can make this a fast half day or a full day of amazing riding, depending on your preference.

The route is lift dependent, so make sure they are running before you head off. The route also goes pretty high up into the mountains so check out the weather forecast before you charge out!

Epic

Hard

44km

917m

2914m

6-7 Hours

IGN 3528
Morzine

Start Point

Start in Morzine.

If you can blag a lift/shuttle to the end of the road at Chalet des Mines D'Or, then you save yourself the first 330m of the climb......

Montriond

Morzine

1554

les Gets

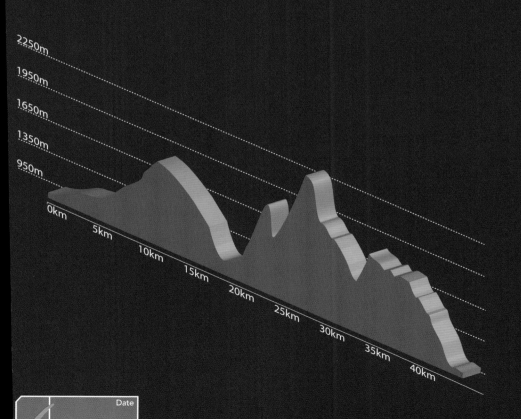

2250m
1950m
1650m
1350m
950m

0km   5km   10km   15km   20km   25km   30km   35km   40km

	Date
	Time

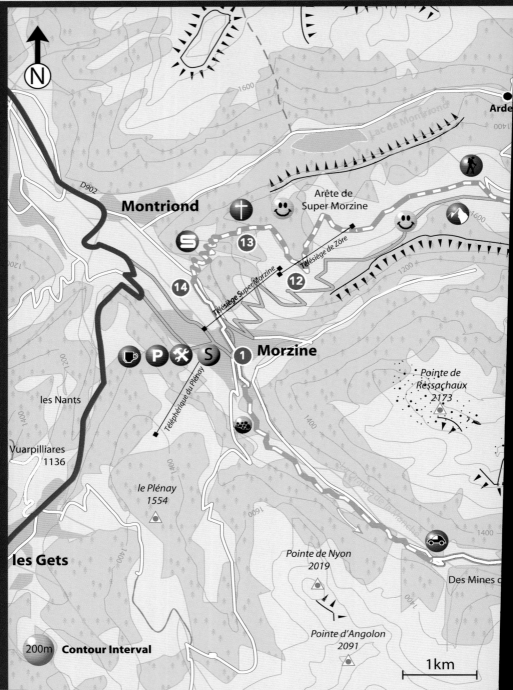

N

Montriond

Arête de
Super Morzine

Arde

Lac de Montriond

1600

D902

1600

13

Télesiège de Zöre

14

12

Télesiège Super Morzine

Morzine

1

les Nants

Vuarpilliares
1136

le Plénay
1554

Pointe de
Ressachaux
2173

Pointe de Nyon
2019

Pointe d'Angolon
2091

Des Mines d

les Gets

Téléphérique du Plénay

200m **Contour Interval**

1km

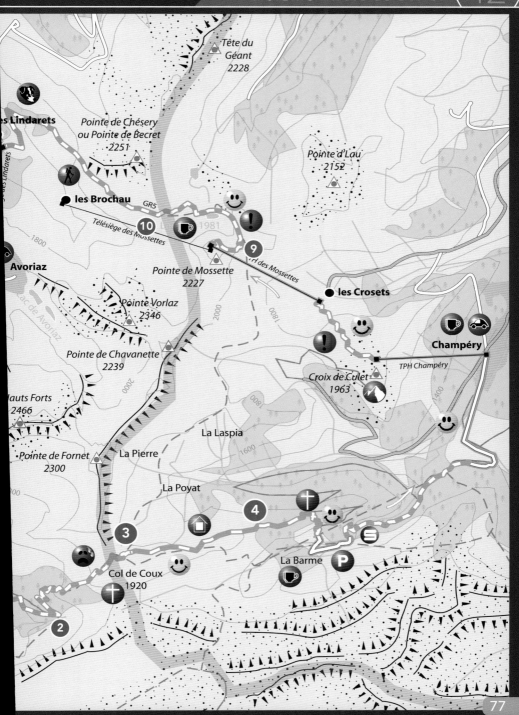

es Lindarets

Pointe de Chésery
ou Pointe de Becret
2251

Tête du
Géant
2228

Pointe d'Lau
2152

les Brochau

GR5

Télésiège des Mossettes

10

Les ... 1981

9

..rt des Mossettes

les Crosets

Avoriaz

Pointe de Mossette
2227

Pointe Vorlaz
2346

Champéry

TPH Champéry

Pointe de Chavanette
2239

Croix de Culet
1963

auts Forts
2466

La Laspia

Pointe de Fornet
2300

La Pierre

La Poyat

4

3

Col de Coux
1920

2

La Barme

P

La Barme

Route Description

① The Grind upwards

Head out of the southern end of Morzine, where the road starts for Avoriaz. Take the small stone track alongside la Dranse. Follow this, climbing steadily, until the track joins the road at l'Erigne Derriere. Turn right here and continue to climb until the road stops at Pt 1340m, (the turning for the Chalet des Mines d'Or).

② Singletrack climb

Here is the unavoidable climb - head off on the left hand of the stone tracks and climb steadily upwards to where the track meets the Torrent de Chardonniere. Take the singletrack here climbing up to the left, and follow this round the switchbacks and through the woodland all the way to the Col de Coux. The climbing is technical, and you're going to need a strong pair of legs to be able to ride all of this.

③ Singletrack traverse

From the col head down the rough track for 300m. At this point a small singletrack heads off to the right, (part of a red cycle route). Follow this as it traverses across the hillside, some great technical riding with the odd rock step . The track takes you through to the small farm at Pt. 1816, where the red route heads off down the track and into the valley base.

④ Berroi ridge singletrack

Up along the line of the ridge you will see a cross sticking out. Follow the singletrack leading up to this, and admire the views - and the drop to your left - from the cross. From this point you now have 220m of some of the best singletrack descent in the area. Twisty, rocky, rooty switchback trail will test your riding skills as you head down along the ridge and through the delightful woods to Pt. 1619, where you come out onto a small parking area and a road.

⑤ Rocky blast

The trail ahead of you looks inviting, but at the time of writing has a no cycling sign at the top of it. Take the road and follow it to the right until you get to the collection of small buildings that include the spot where the refuge de la Barme, stood. Time for a break? Pick up the signs for the red cycle route again, and follow the grassy track heading east past the buildings. Cross over the stream and follow a steep rocky switchbacked track under the cliffs of La Braye until you meet the road.

⑥ Road descent & lift access

Once you meet the road, turn right onto it and follow it swiftly downhill through Grand Paradis and onwards into Champery. The lift is on the right, with some pleasant cafes and restaurants right next to the lift. Take the main Champery telecabin upwards to access the return part of the route.

⑦ Les Crosets DH

Once at the top of the lift access, head out of the lift station and across (quick down and climb back up) to the top of the Les Croset downhill course, Croix de Culet. The downhi course is a real blast - some wonderful berms and sharp rocky descents that soon throw you out into Les crosets where you can stop at a refuge or access other lifts. If you have time, head back up on the lift and do the Les Crosets course as many times as you want!

 Les Mossette lift & Grande Conche DH Course

When you've had your fill of the Les Crosets DH, head up on the Les Mossette left to Pt 2277m. For those of you, who know just how much riding you still have yet to do, but who still want more, then you can always head down the ridge and do laps on the Grand Conche Swiss National Course, alternating between the old and the new start points. Just don't look down when you're on the first switchbacks on the new start!

 Rocky downhill

From the top of the lift head down by a choice of two wide rocky tracks towards Lac Vert, either way which gives a great blast. From the junction, take the track to the right of Lac Vert, then reaching the small refuge at the end of the lake Pt. 1981m.

 GR5

Take the track to the right of the refuge and climb up towards the Col de Chésery Pt 1992. From here follow the GR5 down and along towards Les Lindarets, enjoying some really fast descent here. Take care where the track splits in some places for walkers and bikers. Once you drop into Les Lindarets, head up for the top car park and the lift stations.

 Les Lindarets lift

Take the Lindarets lift to arrive above Avoriaz. Head right, joining the road by the entrance to Avoriaz. Follow this down past the Col de Joux Plane, and a little further down head right onto tracks along the Super Morzine Arête to reach the top of the Zore lift.

 Montriond singletrack

From the top of the Zore lift, take the small singletrack running along the arête to Le Col de la Croix des Combes at Pt 1637. The riding is fast and flowing, with some technical steps and switchbacks down through the woods. Pass through the small wire gate by the cross, and follow the singletrack running WNW through open ground and down into woods. The trail is super fast and straight here, bringing you and some very hot brakes down onto a wider track a few hundred metres lower!

 Montriond stone track

Once on this main track head uphill for the last climb of the route. A hundred metres uphill (not vertically!) you reach a junction. Take the right fork here and head down for the final amazing descent - steep, fast rocky ground, with some fabulous wide switchbacks to power around. Eventually, halfway between Montriond and Morzine you will reach a road inbetween a collection of newly built houses at l'Ele.

 Homeward bound

Turn left onto the road, and climbing slightly, follow it back into Morzine.

Summary

A wonderful and quick 'get away for a while' loop from the heart of Morzine. If you have a couple of hours to spare and want to go and do some riding 'off the back' , then you'll enjoy this ride. The route has a combination of some suprisingly tough climbs with some technical singletrack and some descents that are simply just going to make you giggle!

The lift takes you straight out of Morzine and in no time at all you are on the ridge and riding in the footsteps of the great names of the Tour de France. Follow this with some cheeky riding from the Col de Joux Plane and fast swooping descents under the Nyon lift to create a delectable riding mix.

Morzine	
Blast/ Expert	
Hard	**3**
15 km	
160 m	
690 m	
1 - 3 hr	
IGN 3528	

Start Point

Start in Morzine at the Le Plenay lift station. Take the lift up and on exiting go directly up the wide stone track heading uphill in front of you.

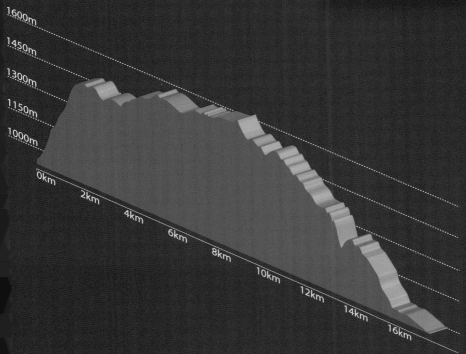

Date

Time

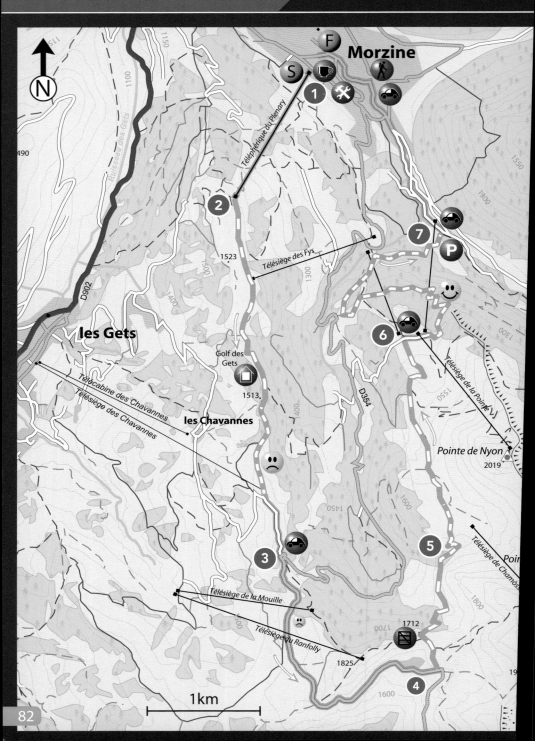

Morzine

les Gets

les Chavannes

Golf des Gets
1513.

Téléphérique du Plenary

Télésiège des Fys

Télécabine des Chavannes

Télésiège des Chavannes

Télésiège de la Pointe

Pointe de Nyon
2019

Télésiège de la Mouille

Télésiège du Ranfolly

Télésiège de Chamos

1712

1825

N

1km

1 Le Plenay Lift

Take the lift up. The hard bit of the route.....

2 Le Plenay Ridge

Head out of the lift station and climb up the rough stone track towards the cafe at the edge of the golf course - probably a bit early to stop just yet! So follow the track along the ridge, riding along a wide track with some steep roller coaster climbs on it. Arrive at Pt 1513m.

3 Tour de France Road Climb

Continue up along the road on a steady climb around the back of the Tete du Vuargne passing the decals and names of the Tour de France riders that swept through here just a few years back. Continue on to the Chalet du Col.

4 Singletrack descent on the edge!!

At the east end of the lake head north on a rough grass and stone track (turn off left by a small collection of buildings) for a gentle climnb. Go through a small gate at the col and follow the track heading northwards. The riding is now steep, rocky singletrack, with some short sharp climbs and rock steps that will test your trials skills. The drop off to the left of the trail will help you to concentrate!

5 Water stop & Rocky blast

The trail spits you out with a final steep section. Take the short steep climb up to the right and then the rough stone track. Pass to the left of the reservoir and small buildings. There is a water fountain just by the building if you need a refill. Continue to follow the wide stone track down all the way into Les Raverettes for a great fun blast back.

6 Pre Favre singletrack descent

Turn right on the small road and car park area and head up to La Combe where a track heads off to the left. The track then descends via some lovely switchbacks down and under the Nyon lift and traverses across the hill to the left. At a small track junction (straigh on to meet a road) head down and right and take the swoopimg and fast singletrack descent past Pille to the car park area at the bottom of the ski run.

7 La Dranse stone track

Head leftwards along through the car park and go across the bridge on the left at the end of th car park, just by the sign for the Cascade de Nyon.

Follow the wide stone track running alongside la Dranse until it spits you out onto the road at the SE end of Morzine. Turn left and climb up the hill and follow the road along to get to the Plenay Lift and into town for a refreshment stop.

Châtel

Morgins

Tête de Linga

Tête du Géant

Pointe du Chésery

Introduction

At the heart of Portes du Soleil is the Châtel Valley and the small towns of Châtel and Morgins. These small towns can easily be used as a pleasent bike base in order to explore the whole area. From June to September, the many cable cars and chairlifts in the area will take you up to join hundreds of kilometres of trails and walking paths.

Châtel is home to a several Bike Parks specifically designed for the dedicated rider. There are slalom and XC trails as well as DH courses providing a ride to suit everyone. Super Châtel is the place to go if you want more hardcore DH and is being superbly developed with plans to open up many more areas for exciting MTB riding.

From Châtel you can reach the top of the new Pre la Joux bike park by the Pierre Longue and or Rochassons lifts. This area offers nine purely free-ride trails, some new North Shore routes and a 4X track plus a dirt-zone track as well as access to XC trails with amazing views all round.

Châtel is also home to the 'Fantasticable' a completely amazing zip wire ride along two cables which run hundreds of metres above the valley and across it above the Pres La Joux area; a must for the daring adventurer. There is also a Luge run and a small Devalkart at Pres la Joux plus a 9 hole golf course to add even more to the long list of activities you can find in Châtel.

Getting there

To get to Châtel follow the same flight routine as for Les Gets and Morzine and you can still get transfers from the airport for a little higher price as it is about an hour further into the hills. If you are travelling by car, start by following the same route from Geneva.

Follow the N3 motorway which becomes the N5 to Thonon Les Bains following the side of Lake Geneva North easterly direction. At Thonon Les Bains, take the D907 and look out for signposts for an easterly turn to Abondance on the D22. Keep on the D22 all the way to Châtel village just by the Swiss border.

Local Services

As Châtel is developing it's biking facilities so the shops and accommodation are developing too. Accommodation is abundant as the winter season chalets and hotels open for the summer season.

Food

In Châtel, the traditional festivals of food, wine and dance run through the summer months and the local cuisine to be tried for its regional authenticity is fondue and potee.

In the centre of the village for some great food are the restaurants of Le Grizzli on Route des Vonnes and Le Perrier among others, all offering a great selection of local cuisine.

If you're just after pizzas or snacks there is a large list of places to choose from including La Flambee and La Grange. Just for snacks and bar meals there are many snack bars and pubs which don't mind you leaving your bike by your table so long as you have a cool beer at the same time. As with most areas in the Portes du Soleil, there are many shops selling local produce as well as two supermarkets, The Sherpa and The Vival in Châtel itself. As ever, there is a disproportional amount of bars to frequent after a long day riding.

Accommodation

There are many hotels in Châtel which welcome mountain bikers including the Chalet d'Alizee right in the centre of town and La Ferme de l'Auberge down in the Pres La Joux area closer to the new bike park.

There are also several smaller accommodation providers and an Alpine camp site: Camping l'Oustalet which is surprisingly close to the town centre.

Chalet l'Hermitage sleeps 17 and is one of the many picturesque wood and stone chalets available for reasonable prices and can be telephoned on 0870 7700408 for reservations.

Les Perce Niege is also a great chalet located just near the camping area. They cater for groups upto 6 with very reasonable rates.

There is a central accommodation booking office for Châtel called the Châtel Tour which you can call for information on 0450733022.

Bike Shops & Hire

As the village is small there is not much in the way of good bike shops, so stock up with essentials before you arrive is our advice. The people are very friendly and will do all they can to accommodate mountain bikers. With bike-wash facilities available at some but not all places of accommodation, it's worth checking out what you'll get before booking.

There is one great little bike shop in Châtel, just opposite the plaza where you catch the shuttle bus to Pre La Joux. The shop has all the basic parts and hires bikes out in the summer. You can get repairs done here too. For more information check out the Tourist information web site which also gives links to local service providers.

Vertical Horizons, right next to the camping site is mainly an outdoor shop but does bike hire and most basic repairs.

Getting There

From Morzine

Drive towards Montriond along the D229. At a large biggish roundabout, head back up right towards the Lac de Montriond. Drive past this and on up the alpine switchbacks to the goat mad village of Les Lindarets. Go through the village and park at the bottom of the lift stations.

From the Châtel Valley

Drive south west up the valley from Châtel (direction Très Les Pierres) to the bottom of the lift station at Pré La Joux. Park here and take the Télésiège Pierres Longues and then the Télésiège de Rochassons to the top.

Pré La Joux No1

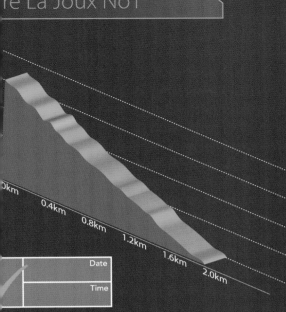

0km 0.4km 0.8km 1.2km 1.6km 2.0km

	Date
	Time

Les Lindarets / Crête des Rochassons

Downhill — DH

Moderate — 2

2.75 km

570 m

10 -25 mins

IGN 3528 ET Morzine

Pré La Joux No 2

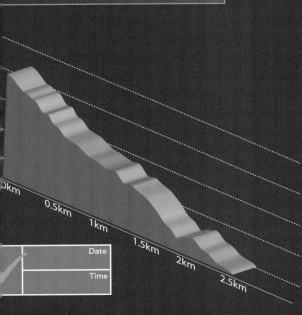

0km 0.5km 1km 1.5km 2km 2.5km

	Date
	Time

Les Lindarets / Crête de Rochassons

Downhill — DH

Hard — 3

2.75 km

570 m

10-30 mins

IGN 3528 ET Morzine

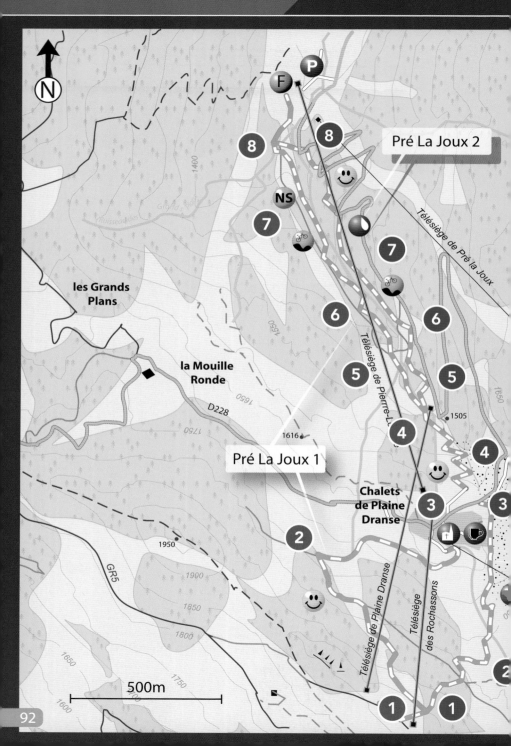

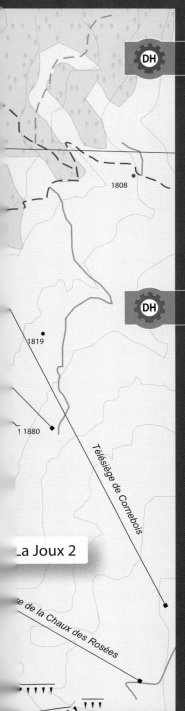

Summary: Pré La Joux No 1

The Pre La Joux DH1 is a very fast but not too technical track on narrow trails. The track is prone to mud, so its well worth avoiding it if its been raining for a few days.

This is a track good for the first run of a Pres la Joux day to warm you up ready for some more serious riding.

If you need a break at some point in the day there are plenty of restaurants and bars scattered around the slopes including a great bike-friendly restaurant at the top of the Pierre Longues lift.

Summary: Pré La Joux No 2

The recently developed Châtel Bike Park at Pres Le Joux offers a selection of high quality and enjoyable routes at all grades. Development continues on here as they add more trails to both sides of the mountain. The Pré La Joux DH2 offers a more technical combination than the DH1 track, this can be a great challenge with mixed ground and some potentially good jumps.

The tracks which the lower stage of this hill provides look like they are all the same, but there are several variations to be tried out. Two contrasting top trails are described with the two different lower down routes in this guide giving you 4 for the price of 2! And if you're feeling really brave, you can also take in the North Shore near the bottom of these runs. Full body armour advised!

If you don't like the sound of all that, the most gentle, but longest way down to the start of the lower level here is the Green Panoramic trail signposted from the top.

DH Pré La Joux No 1

Start

From the top of the Les Lindarets lift: Télésiège de la Chaux Fleurie go straight on to the large wooden sign for the new Châtel bike park of Pre la Joux.

From the top of the Télésiège des Rochassons look right for the same big wooden sign and roll down to it.

1 Bike Park Sign

At the big wooden Pre la Joux Bike Park sign looking straight down and you'll see a dauntingly steep black run on lose scree and mud. Don't worry! Look right to the gravely fire road and head down that instead. Keep heading down checking your brakes as you remember this is a track shared with pedestrians.

2 Fire Road

After a few minutes, meet up with a wide fire road which weaves you down to join another dropping in from the left. Tackle a very rocky and muddy band round to the right and speed up again for a blast down to the road at Chalets de Plaine Dranse.

3 Rock Chapel

Look back left here to a small rock chapel with a mini climbing wall and a metal cross. If you look up right you can check out the zip wire flyers screaming their way down the valley. Head down to the Télésiège du Rochassons. Look to the right of the lift station for a blue VTT sign.

4 'Blue and Roc'

Follow winding singletrack down the open hill into the woods. Following quite steeply now, watch out for deceptively fast switchbacks skirting the trees. Look out for the last two technical switchbacks and stay to the centre of the track as it drops more steeply with trees to your left. Wet rocks here mean you need careful brake use as you float over them bearing left as you come to a rocky drop into a tight right hander before the trail levels out a bit.

5 Fast mini table top

Head along undulating great fast singletrack trying not to lose speed on the mud and look out for drainage gullies. As you come out into the open, pick up speed and look ahead as you quickly come up on a small table top with a chicken run to the left. Look out for a couple of deep drainage gullies across the track with the last one jumpable as you speed to a grassy junction signposted ahead to for the Red DH 'Ric et Rack'. Turn right to the fire road.

6 Interdit au Pied Pas

At the fire track turn left briefly then right to go slightly back on yourself skirting below tarmac road which heads over the river. Just before you cross the river look out for a small VTT sign which says Blue 1 and 'interdit au pied pas' pointing to the start of a new trail. Follow this down on fantastic newly buil narrow track running along the left side of the river. Getting good speed on undulating singletrack, beware of the tiny bridges over drainage gullies!

Pré La Joux No 2

1 Bike Park Sign

Facing the Bike Park Board opposite the top of the lift, look to your right. Follow the sign to a steep, rocky fire track. Follow this until it brings you round to the left with a VTT sign pointing to a red DH alternative off right. Down this a change of terrain, has you pumping your brakes and sliding down more steeply on a muddy run wriggling down a rutted grassy slope.

2 Stony Gully

Bearing right again, use your technical prowess as the track quickly becomes narrow and stony through a gully. Zig zagging down the field now, head right towards a rocky outcrop - avoiding the cows! Becoming very steep and technical the track takes you all the way down to the east side of the village of Chalets de Plane Dranse. Join a gravely track and roll fast down to the lift station for another DH run in the Pre La Joux area below.

3 'Blue & Roc' DH

From the right side of the lower Télésiège des Rochassons station, look for VTT sign for the 'Blue and Roc' DH track. With an off-camber start, you can pick up a fair bit of speed. A short stretch brings you to another fast corner round to the right where the gravel checks your back wheel. So the less braking the better.

4 Rocky Floater

Go wide at the next berm, then try to line yourself up for the middle of the track in order to float over slippy and uneven rocks. Edge to the left side to drop down into a tight right hander at speed.

5 Fast Track

Then its left again for a fast stony track which becomes even narrower as your speed increases. If you edge to the right here you can catch a small table top and dirt jump which bring you to an open field. Ahead is the Red graded 'Ric et Rac' track often closed due to saturation. Go right, along the fire road, straight across and over the river to the trees. To the right is a small section of North Shore but look for a wooden VTT sign pointing you down into the woods on your left. Drop into a winding dirt track prone to mud and pop over the roots taking a line on the right.

6 Rolling Jumps / Real Fun

This short non technical section is made more interesting with rolling jumps to your right. Watch you don't miss them by speeding along the fast wide chicken runs to the left.

Pick up speed as you drop deeper into the woods. Take a wide ride around big grippy berms and switchbacks.

After the last view of the road, take a central line and look out for a precarious small wooden plank over a very deep small gully as you speed out of the woods underneath the lift cables. With a quick left turn look out for a fork with a sign for 'shore' to the left.

DH Pré La Joux No 1

(7) Oh the mud!

Keep up your speed as you have a roller coaster ride through a very muddy section. Look out for roots and more small wooden bridges over the worst muddy sections and gullies. Without any turning you can lose a lot of speed in more mud, so look for the driest ruts and pump your peddles through them.

(8) Final twist

Just as you pick up speed again look ahead to a quick right and left switchback which drops you in to the last stretch. With a last short blast, come out to the fire road and head across the meadow to your right.

Don't forget, there's a bike wash down here for real muddy bums on a bogging day to help out the lift attendants.

Turn right at the fire road crossing the meadow on the left and staying to the left side of the lift to head straight back up for more!

DH Pré La Joux No 2

(7) North Shore Area

Bearing round to the right, there is some rooty ground to join back up with the exit of the North Shore area! If you venture into theNorth Shore you are up against some short sections varying from 2ft wide to about 10ft high. You'll find this, and smaller technical rises will all test your bike skills and balance but, hopefully not, your holiday insurance!

Back left into the trees, take the series of small jumps and keep your speed to help tackle the next undulating section of rooty muddy ground. After a final steep switchback, come up a small rise and peddle for a minute as the track crosses over the river on a new wooden bridge.

(8) Fire Road

Turn right at the fire road which crosses the meadow on the left and staying to the left side of the lift to head straight back for more!

Singletrack

mountain bike magazine

Issue 25 December 2005
Still £3.75

www.singletrackworld.com

Getting There

Châtel is the most northerly of the Bike Parks in Portes du Soleil. If you're staying in the Châtel Valley its easy to get to, if not it involves a long drive round from Morzine via Jean Des Alpes and Abondonce.

Alternatively

There is a bus service from the Pré La Joux side of Lindarets into Châtel. This means you can lift hop from Morzine to Avoriaz, ride down into Les Lindarets, take the lift up sto the top of Les Lindarets, ride down into Pré La Joux and catch the shuttle bus to Châtel. Don't be late back though, or you'll be finding that you have to get your credi card out for an impromptu nights stay.

nne Caro

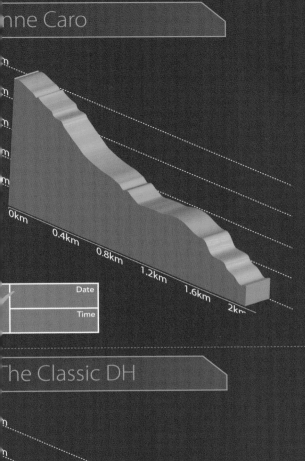

	Date
	Time

Châtel	
Downhill	DH
Extreme	4
2.6 km	
495 m	
5 - 20 mins	
IGN 3528 Carte Suisse Monthey1284	

he Classic DH

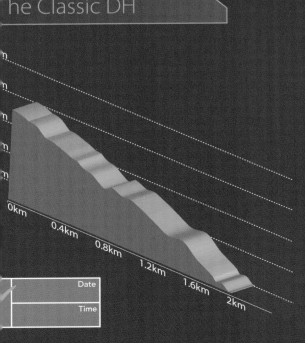

	Date
	Time

Châtel	
Downhill	DH
Hard	3
2.25 km	
410 m	
5 - 15 mins	
IGN 3528 Carte Suisse Monthey1284	

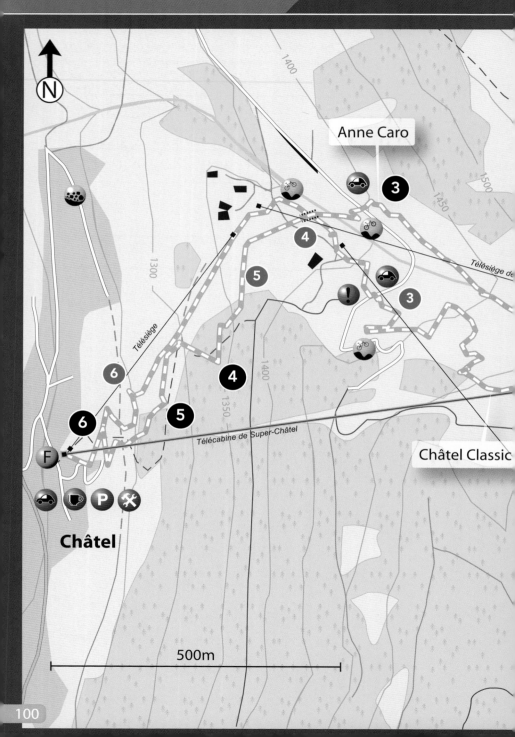

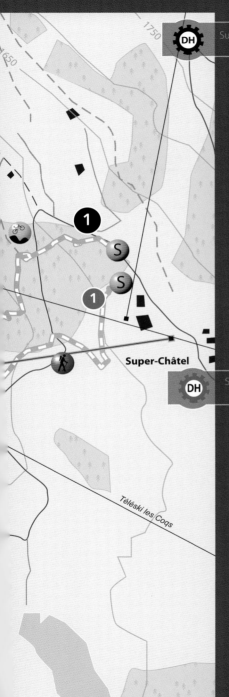

Summary: Anne Caro

This is a full on heavy-duty track. When it's not being super fast, then it's in the trees and proper steep. Be very careful down here as one minute your pinning it along the flat and then without warning you are round a corner and heading down hill- a lot! This track is mainly made up of singletrack with the odd root section thrown in to keep things spicy.

Start

From the centre of Châtel head up the Super Châtel lift. When in the top lift station, exit the building at the rear and turn left. Join the fire road and head down there for about 50 metres to a turning on your left. The trail starts just down there.

Summary: Classic DH

The Classic is an easy to medium level track with varying terrain. This trail includes quite a lot of jumps so it will appeal to the air junkie. All the bigger jumps have chicken runs to keep this track open to the less confident riders as well as the faster more advanced trail heads.

Start

From Châtel head up the Super Châtel lift with your bikes in the cabin! When leaving the top lift station head out the back and turn left. Join the fire road and carry on along there, past the turning on the left. The track starts around 100 metres from the lift.

Anne Caro

 Root Heaven!

From the start there is a small straight leading towards the first root section and a left-hand corner. The roots carry on for a short while and through a right - left switchback. Still on the roots round another right and a small but awkward drop.

Keep high for the easier line. Take the next left but keep to the right on the exit if you want to do the rather large road gap. As with all big jumps it is a good idea to check it out first. This one especially as the run out is really quite short and leads into a left-hand corner very quickly.

2 Tight, steep bends

A short straight before a series of particularly tight and steep s bends. On the second left keep well to the left as it becomes really off camber and you need to make it across the narrow bridge at the bottom.

Into narrow tree section with a right-hander and a straight section (still quite tight), slight right left kink. On exit of the left there is a jump to the left or you can roll round on the right. Here there is a long straight in the open on narrow singletrack.

3 Right-hander & tight drop

As you approach the slight right-hander it does start to get a bit bumpy, then big hip to the left. Depending on how much you hipped it, on the left there is a small drop but don't launch too much as there is only a short landing into a right hander. Go over a small jump on the left, slight right and some weaving singletrack then you're across a bridge and onto a fire road.

4 Boulder Drop

Across the road and there is a big boulder drop on the right or a less technical line on the left. Take this slow at first as it gets quite steep and you have to make a slight right to get across another bridge.

Over a few rocks, slight right left and across a big bridge (this time over another trail). Now faced with the only real break you get and a flat, even slightly uphill, pedalling section. Over the top, turn right, put a few more pedals in and you're back in to the woods.

5 Woods

As you enter the woods it becomes quite narrow once again. Take this with caution, as there is suddenly a tight right left with a small drop. In this section it is the narrowness of the trail and the closeness of the trees that makes it so intense.

Another right, very steep down a couple of rocks and immediately left before hitting a big catch net. A short straight, then right onto a steep bank with a right left kink on it, another right left onto small shoot onto a fire road. Phew!

6 Fire Road

Turn left along the fire road for a short distance, then take a right down a piece of singletrack. Big left with a catch net, weaving singletrack onto another fire road and you're done!

DH Classic DH

1 Start Gate

Head through the start gate and round an easy left onto a flat straight. Then 3 jumps, left is the easy line and the bigger jump is on the right (careful for the flat landing). The trail continues along the flat for a little further, round a slight left into right hand berm. A short straight including a couple of small rollable jumps, then a small kink takes you onto the first fire-road crossing.

2 Double Rollers

Long left / right including a couple of really small rollable doubles and then you have a choice of smooth left line or big take off to the right, really flat landing on this one. I prefer the left line as the landing off the big jump just feels so wrong. Either way you have a small straight into a right hand berm which is the start of a long section of corners including several small rollable jumps.

3 Have a go!!

After the switchbacks and the ensueing straight the trail opens up over a small jump and a slight left. Slight right takes you into the people's favourite section. Two jumps on the right hand side, both land into a small bomb hole but the jump on the far right is a bit longer to the landing.

You can roll round the left hand side but the jump in the middle is easier than it looks and worth a go once you have had a look. Then from there into tight right round a big tree, left berm and another fire-road crossing.

4 Under the bridge

Off the fire-road into a series of fairly tight switchbacks down to another fire-road. Straight over to a big open right left, down to some trees and a fairly tight right through the trees and under a bridge (Anne Caro track).

5 Speed the bumps

Out into the open and over a reasonable sized double, open left-hander onto the side of a fire road. Long straight section down the side of the fire-road, fast as you like.

This can be quite bumpy and the faster you go the scarier it gets. A couple of small bus stops off the side slow things down a bit before you head off right onto a narrow piece of singletrack. If you want to finish with the duel track look out for a little turn off to your right.

6 Ready for another?

Which ever way you choose to finish continue heading down to get back to the lift.

Now back to the top for another go on that jump!

Corbeau Blast

Châtel Valley

Summary

Get out of town for a while and blow the cobwebs away.

This trail is a fantasic mixed blast, with a combination of singletrack and wider fire road as well as a bit of minor road and lots of not very technical downhill. A good ride to do as a quickie in the morning or afternoon, or just for a brief diversion from the Châtel and Pres La Joux DH and North Shore riding.

With great views and not too much up hill peddling, this trail is also the perfect outing for your competent riding children or VTT newbies. The added bonus of crossing the border into Switzerland over two valleys also provides an excursion to savour.

Super
Châtel Lift

Blast

Moderate

14 km

300 m

460 m

1 -2 hrs

IGN 3528
Carte Suisse
Monthey1284

Getting There

From the junction in the centre of Châtel (confusing signage here), follow the tarmac road up the hill to the Télécabine de Super Châtel.

Turn back on yourself to the right at the next junction, to find the bottom lift station, which should be only 100m further along the road. Take the lift up to the top at 1660m.

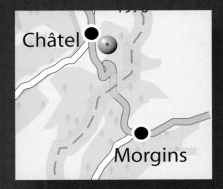

Start Point

Télécabine de Super Châtel

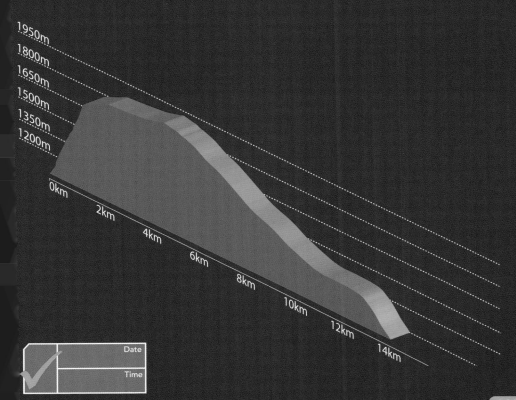

	Date
	Time

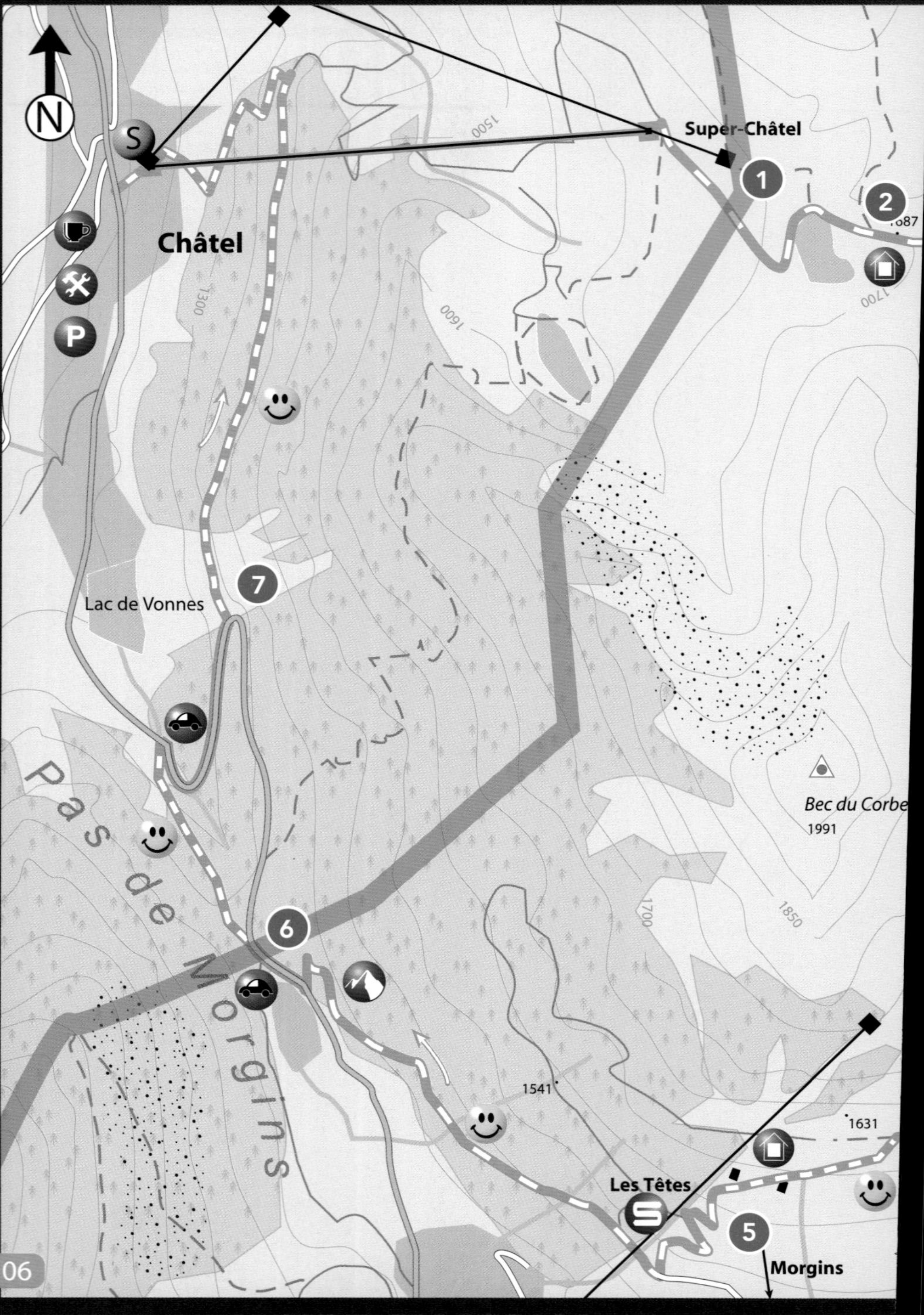

N

S

Super-Châtel

① Châtel

②

1687

1700

1500

1300

1600

😊

Lac de Vonnes

⑦

🚗

😊

Pas de Morgins

⑥

🚗

⛰

Bec du Corbe

1991

1850

1700

1541

😊

1631

🏠

😊

Les Têtes

S

⑤

Morgins

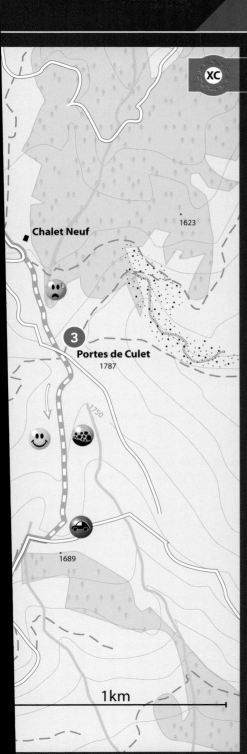

Chalet Neuf

1623

3

Portes de Culet
1787

1750

1689

1km

Corbeau Blast

1 Super Châtel Lift

From the top of the Super Châtel lift, head to your right for a short up hill climb on fire track. This takes you over the invisible Swiss border to a fork in the trail.

Go left, then left again, taking the trail down to a small lake. Next, skirt around the left side of the lake at Le Grollet, passing a couple of pretty little chalets.

2 Chalets

Follow the trail down to a T junction, with a minor road and turn right. Head uphill for a short section, until you come to a tight right hand corner. Just after passing Chalet Neufas turn around this corner and on your left is a piece of singletrack. Turn on to this for a short but steep uphill section.

If you want to avoid heading straight up the hill, you can stay on the minor road and weave a bit more slowly upward.

3 Portes de Culet

At Portes de Culet 1787m the track and road meet up again. Look straight across the road to your right, and turn on to a rocky bit of singletrack heading down the hill Rolling down to 1689m, the trail meets up with another minor road, follow this around the left hand bend for only a few metres until taking a turn off right to singletrack again .

If you miss this turn by going too fast, you can roll 100m further down on the road to the next piece of singletrack on your right and take this instead. This meets up with the missed track at a junction of trails.

(4) Trails Junction

Continue the loop by turning down hill and taking the left trail to a fast widening piece of trail. This quickly passes two chalets, where you tackle a steepening slope.

Where the trail turns into tarmac, follow the minor road down hill steeply and zig zag between the cluster of chalets that is the Les Têtes. Remember to lookout for cars on the tight bends as you come down to 1485m.

(5) Switchbacks on road

The road turns onto a final switchback taking you right again and heading you toward the Pas Du Morgins. Heading still downwards slightly and skirting around the contour of the hill, pop out of the trees briefly and look back over your left shoulder for fine views of the village of Morgins.

Skirt the woods with the trees to your right, and check your brakes as you come to a quick left hand switchback which traverses above and around a small rocky outcrop. This takes you down to another tarmac road.

Turn right here and go along the road for the last few metres, heading slightly uphill, to a large wooden sign for the Pas de Morgins. Now you're on the French/Swiss border again.

(6) French / Swiss Border

Here you are half in France and half in Switzerland and can look down into to both the Châtel and Morgins valleys.

Turn left off the road heading in the Châtel direction and go on to the section of singletrack heading down the hill (not the section of singletrack heading up hill just before it). Speed onwards to a fork where you turn right to ride along a tarmac road.

The road quickly bears round to the left with you heading up slightly. Take the track to the left on the tight right bend.

(7) Lac de Vonnes

Heading off the road, contour above the Lac de Vonnes, staying on the uphill side and heading slightly west, to arrive under the lift cables.

At the next fork go left, to join the very last section of the Super Châtel DH. This pops out on to the bottom fire road where you turn left and whiz all the way back down to the lift station

bikefaX

Tour du Pointe de L'Au

Morginss

Summary

The Tour de Pointe L'Au consists mainly of broad fire track interspersed with some lovely singletrack sections. With lots of ups, which can be quite challenging, and lots of downs this tour is a true traditional cross country ride.

From start to finish there are breathtaking views all round. The ride takes in two valleys in two countries as you cross and re-cross the Swiss border.

Starting in the quieter village of Morginss, you will see few other riders on this route. If you want a gentle day off, away from the crowds, then this is the ride to do.

Morgins

Classic

Moderate ②

18 km

590 m

550m

2.5 hrs

Carte Suisse
Monthey 1284
Val D'Illiez 1304

Getting There

From Les Gets and Morzine

You can get to Morgins by a long drive around the mountain via Montriond, St Jaen D'Alpes and Abondance. This scenic, but rather slow journey takes just over an hour.

OR

Lift hop over using the lifts at Morzine, Avoriaz and Les Crosets. Allow about an hour for this. If you do this, you'll come into the Pointe L'Au tour about half way round at the 'Pas du Portes du Soleil'.

Start Point

From the centre of Morgins, take the télésiège steeply up to the top (approx 10-15mins). The summit is often in the clouds, so be prepared for some much cooler conditions as you approach the top station.

This lift has one of the nicest lift attendants in the Portes du Soleil and he also happens to speak great english, so say hello from us.

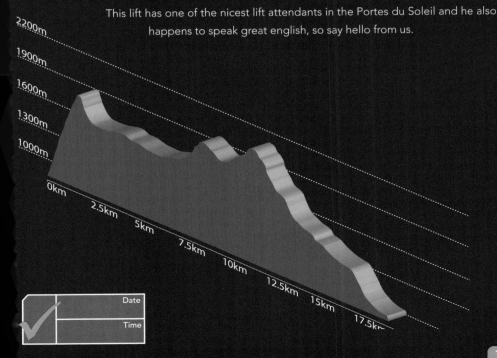

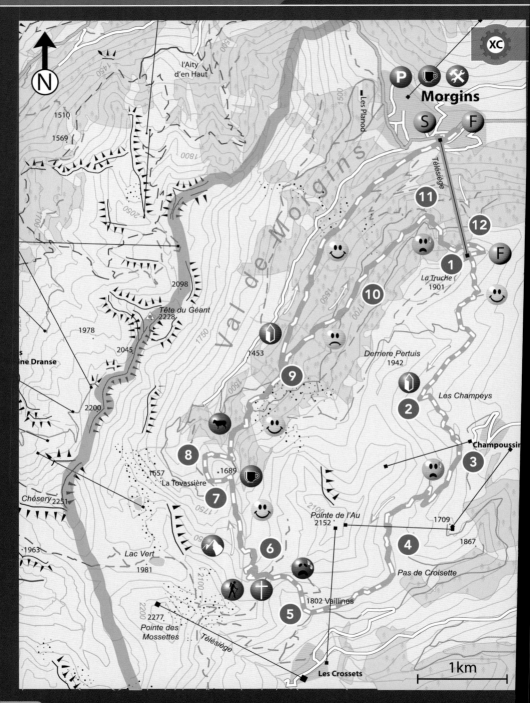

Tour du Pointe de L'Au

1 Top Lift Station

There are several VTT signs here. Look for a yellow one pointing toward Les Crosets (2 hours 40 mins).

It is often very cloudy at the top of the lift station, so get your bearings before setting off. The cloud tends to clear quickly as soon as you start the descent but its worth making sure you are on the right side of the mountain first!

Go straight on out of the lift and drop over the top of the hill directly away from the station following a lovely piece of grassy singletrack down the hill. Get your bearings before heading down into the abyss, as it's steepness and damp grass can be a tricky combination.

Heading downwards, you bear right and ride under another set of cables to a crossroads at 1717m where you turn right. Continue on, bearing left at a fork in the trail This takies you uphill slightly to Les Brochasses.

2 Wooden sign to Les Champeys

Follow the sign to Les Champeys and gently contour the hill before hitting a quick switchback and heading through the village. Continue cruising round with gently flowing downhill, and follow the widening track on the left side of a small lake.

3 Track Junction

At 1687m the track joins another. Go right for the start of the biggest uphill part of the trail. Have a quick breather and get your legs ready as there's a total of 230m to climb ahead!

4 Big Climb

Staying on this fire track, pump your way uphill to take a right turn at the first big switchback and then go left at the second switchback. This brings you up to 1800m. From here comfortably contour around the southern side of the ridge below to the beautiful Point de L'Au.

Pass a small wooden hut on your left and head up to the Pas de Croisettes where the track joins another. Here head straight on to a section of easy downhill. Head right, then right again at the small junction. Continue all the way to Vaillime, catching your breath before the next uphill section.

5 Junction

Head right at the next junction on to a smaller track, and with good traction begin the climb. The track heads straight up the hill or for a quick breather where you can take the next right which wriggles back to the left and up. Whichever way you choose to take, both routes join up at the top of the ridge for dramatic views of the Alpine crags in the distance.

6 Track Junction

At a junction of trails, go left to follow an old semi-tarmac road which zigzags down the hill. Don't turn off this fast track, but keep an eye out for farm vehicles as you race round the bends to a very tight left hander with a track off to the right.

Keep to the left to pass the beautifully carved wooden cross at the Pas du Portes du Soleil. The track finally brings you down to 1690m and the Mountain Restaurant of La Torvassiere. This is an excellent lunch stop and a grand place to just sit and stare at the mountains for a while.

7 Restaurant of La Torvassiere.

This spot gives remarkable views of the beautiful valley and waterfalls beside the

steep ridge of the Tête du Géant. There is also a massive yellow pole sign for walkers saying 1hour 20 to Morgins. The VTT sign here points you to the right and down the side of the restaurant in the direction of Morgins.

8 Singletrack

Follow the sign to a little used singletrack through a field full of alpine cows. Head over a little grid at a gap in the electric fence to join a pleasant old piece of singletrack as it makes its way around the woods.

9 Fire Road

Join another fire road and keep following the VTT sign. Looking up to your left is a beautiful view of massive rocky outcrop above very steep grassy slopes. Take a right turn at a junction of fire roads. Head uphill for the sta

Alternative Route

At this point the Tour du Pointe L'Au turns right and battles back up to the top of the lift station to finish with a final blast down the built trails at Morgins. If you don't fancy any more uphill there is an easier finish which takes you quickly and easily straight back down to Morgins

To do this - take the left fork then next right for a fast run back down to Morgins.

The Normal Route

If you want to carry on and take in a final blast at Morgins - keep following the route description.

10 Grands Moilles hill

Riding around and up the Grands Moilles hill, keep following VTT signs on the fire road (reminiscent of those in Wales) up to a fork in the track. Take the right turn and go straight on still heading uphill, though a little more steeply here. Staying on this line, take the next right where the track forks again and you're almost at the top.

11 Sweeping right hand bend

Wriggling up to Pt 1670m, the trail comes around the front of the ridge where you take a quick right to point you directly at the Morgins lift cables. This track takes you under the lift cables then back round to join up with a junction of more trails and fire road at the top of the lift at 1816m.

12 Top Lift Station

From here you can now enjoy a last blast of the day by heading down on the only Morgins downhill trail. This starts behind you to the left or by following the left hand XC trail down the head of the hill and back to the east side of Morgins.

Morgins DH

Morgins

Summary

This trail is one of the easier of the DH trails in Portes du Soleil and a perfect track to get up your speed and practice cornering and jumps. An added benefit to the novice DH rider is that this trail is not so largely used by the top boys and girls, thus giving a little less pressure to those wanting to slowly better themselves.

With the added option of easily getting off the main trail via an old worn fire track, should you find it's all getting too hard, it's a trail suitable for the complete DH beginner or older children. It is not recommended though for very young children, as even though it's graded 'DH easy' it's still very steep.

The track is well worn and steep too, so check your brakes are working properly before setting off and get yourself some padding.

Morgins

Downhill

Moderate

2.75km

500m

10 - 20 mins

Carte Suisse Val D'Illez 1284

Getting There

From the centre of Morgins village take the lift up to La Truche. It can be very cold cloud land up here with poor visibility so prepare yourselves for cooler temperatures.

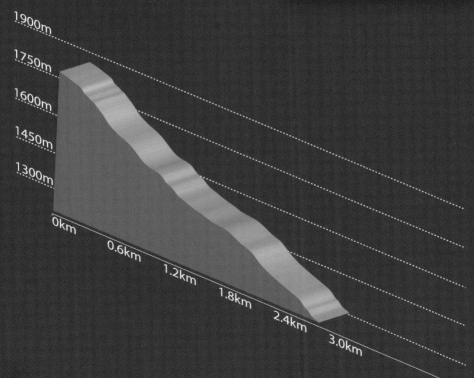

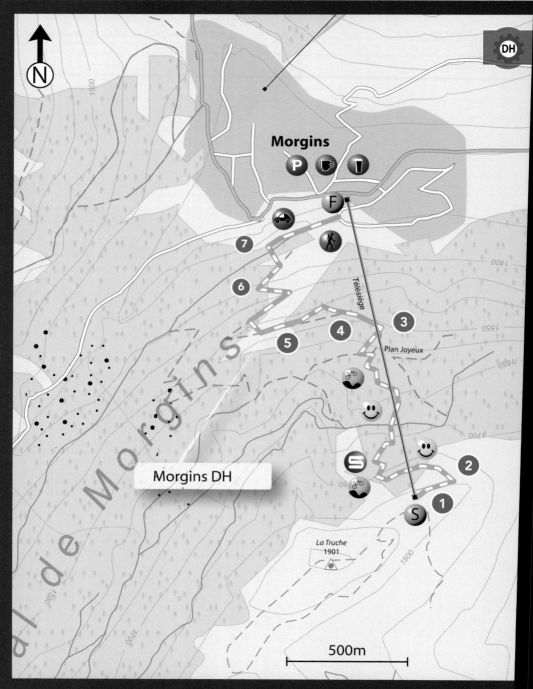

N

Morgins

Morgins DH

Télésiège

Plan Joyeux

La Truche
1901

500m

Morgins DH

① Start

From the top of the télécabine, turn to your left and ride on to a fire road which quickly drops down to the right. This trail starts off weaving back and forth on the old worn fire road with a couple of small switchbacks through water worn grassy tufted ground. Keep on this uneven track until reaching a well maintained big high berm on the right, to drop into the start of the Morgins DH track.

② Steep rocky section

Speed down a very steep rocky part of the track and spoting the kick jumps to your right, head steeply down to reach a junction at a flatter section. Follow the sign to Bonavaux and Morgins DH, going more steeply, then quickly turning off to the right and down a short drop into a steep section of narrow track.

③ Woods

Drop into a steep wooded section, looking out for exposed roots. This section is usually well drained, but can be very slick on the roots. The trail quickly pops you out across the fire road to a couple of easy jumps and berms. The fire road is now on your right hand side as you again pick up speed.

④ Trail Junction

When you reach a split in the trail, take the left side. This runs parallel with the berm hill and makes the most of the on this quite straight forward singletrack sectionl as it becomes very open with several little jumpy bits to play on.

Hop in and out of the woods with a couple of rooty sections either side of a fire road. Hip jumps and a big wide berm bring you back on yourself as you head down the hill for a last little technical section.

⑤ VTT sign on tree

The DH trail itself now pops out on to the steep piste fire road where several little hip jumps and mini berms have been built up. Alternatively, you can go just for the speed by sticking to the fire road here.

If you bailed off the track earlier and you are on the fire road at this point, look for a metal post stuck on a tree. This points you to 'Morgins par la route foristierre' and 'Morgins par la piste VTT'. Follow the VTT sign down, to your right turn if you decide to stay on the fire road.

⑥ Short & Steep

Just before a tight left hand corner in the fire road the DH track drops very steeply for a short section, before joining back up with the fire track again. When this joins up with a wider well maintained fire track, turn right and really pick up some speed.

⑦ Road

This brings you down on to a tarmac road where you turn left heading uphill slightly to get back to Morgins centre.

Les Crosets & Les Lindarets

les Hauts Forts

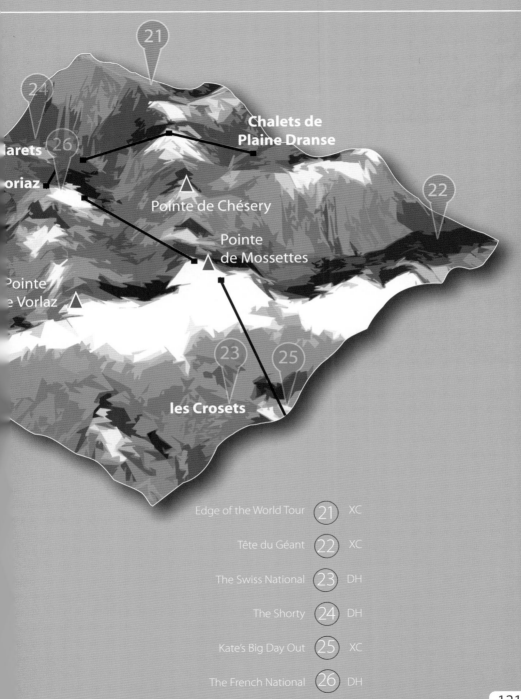

Chalets de
Plaine Dranse

arets

oriaz

Pointe de Chésery

Pointe
de Mossettes

Pointe
e Vorlaz

les Crosets

Both Les Crosets & Les Lindarets are really no more than tiny alpine hamlets with limited facilities and few local services. But do visit them, as they both host some excellent and continually developing mountain bike parks, fantastic DH and a network of marked XC trails.

Les Crosets

Les Crosets is a small, picturesque, family orientated village tucked away just over the Swiss border. Standing at an altitude of 1668m the village lies in a beautiful natural landscape set at the head of a steep mountain valley.

The village hosts an abundance of outdoor activities. For dedicated downhillers, Les Crosets is the site of the Swiss National DH

Course, a ride not to be missed, but only after a good warm up on other trails around. For cross country riders, the area offers great link up routes with the possibility of over 2,000 metres of descending and with careful planning and judicious use of the lifts in the area, very little peddling uphill.

With its winter season being a big success, the area has many chair lifts, gondolas and cable cars of which just two are in use during the summer season, so check their opening time before setting off to this area. The highest point accessible by lifts and local transport in the summer is 2250m. Les Crosets also has its own paragliding school, swimming at Lac Ve and sign posted walks to the Pas de Porte du Soleil, as well as Via Ferrata days out fo those with a good head for heights.

With only 70 full time local inhabitants, Les Crosets is great for those who like to get away from the centre stage of tourism but who still want some amenities. There are many kilometres of marked VTT and DH trails, some of which are officially shared with horse riders and walkers, so don't forget to respect other trail users and you'll go a long way!

Les Lindarets

Just over the Pointe De Chésery to the West of Les Crosets, the slightly quirky hamlet of Les Lindarets has an alpine charm of its own. It is a tiny little place, with the lifts just out of the village uphill from the small cluster of houses and restaurants high up in the mountains.

Known as 'the village of goats', the streets are full of tourists feeding the smelly animals, with specially purchased bags of food. It's a bit like Trafalgar Square, but with goats instead of pigeons! Beware: the goats come before any other traffic in this village!

There are no shops here other than souvenir shops, and unfortunately the nearest bike shop is over the hill in Morginss, so go prepared with most of the tools you could need. For food and drink, there are a couple of hotels and restaurants where you can have a good lunch if caught hungry. There's a good restaurant just at the bottom of the 2 lift stations and plenty more mountain restaurants once you get up the lifts and into the bike areas.

There is also an amazing little refuge run by the Famille Jean-Paul Es-Borrat up at 1980m in the Valle-d'Illiez besides the Lac Verte. Open from the end of June to the end of September they will provide you with wonderful coffee and basic sandwiches. (This refuge sleeps up to 35 and does not have bike store but is great to know of if you're stuck up there for any reason).

Accommodation

Alpine chalets are available in Les Crosets and Les Lindaretss as well as Mountain/alpine huts, hotels and bed and breakfasts. Most bookings for rooms here are based on sharing a double room at 50CHF per night including breakfast. The chalets and mountain huts have a range of standards generally reflected in the price so work out what's best for you/ your group before booking.

Getting there
- To Les Crosets

2 hours from Geneva airport, Les Crosets can be reached by transfer arranged by your accommodation provider. If you are coming by car, the easiest route is via the motorway past Bonneville, Cluses, St Gervais and Chamonix. The road narrows to weave through the mountains through Argentiere over to Trient and across the Swiss border.

Stay on this road until Martigny, where you join the motorway and head north to St Maurice. Here you turn off for Monthey and Troistorrents. At Monthey, turn toward Val-d'Illiez and follow signposts to Les Crosets and the Portes du Soleil. Go up a small winding road which comes to an end at Les Crosets. As with most of Portes du Soleil, the public transport runs all season and time tables can be obtained from most tourist offices.

- To Les Lindarets

Getting to Les Lindarets is a shorter journey. Turn off the motorway from Geneva at Taninges and head to Les Gets and Morzine. From Morzine, head north to Montriond, then up the valley following signs to the Lac De Montriond and thenon to Les Lindaretss.

Local Cuisine

Just up the road from Les Lindarets, and right at the bottom of the Pierre Longues Télésièges, there is a fantastic chalet style hotel and restaurant called Les Marmottes. Here you can get a great omlette for around 8 euros. Just down the hill into the village centre there is a good, if small choice of places to eat, but as this is a real tourist venue, there is not such a warm welcome for those with muddy bums! Taking a packed is lunch is an alternative.

Les Crosets restaurants are more welcoming to muddy bums, and have a wider choice than Les Lindaretss, offering an ample selection of great snacks and meals.

Useful Contacts

For accommodation and local information

www.myswitzerland.com

www.valdillez.com

For detailed weather report links

www.chablais.info

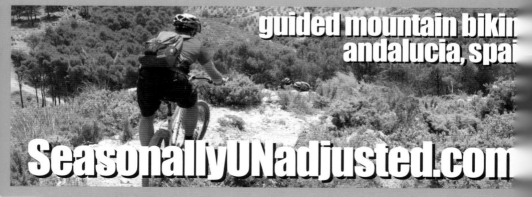

Summary

Here's a trail for those with their wits about them. You'll find all sorts of riding along this route, from wide fire track to rocky steepness and tiny singletrack. Some sections contain sheer drop offs to the side, requiring decisive and skillful riding! Make no mistake, this is a mixed goody bag for the experienced and technical rider only.

Starting at the top of the Lindarets lift system the route makes good use of mechanical ascent, leaving you with fresh legs and time for some racing around the excellent downhill courses in this part of the region.

Skirting around the edge of the steep La Dranse valley, you'll feel at times like you are looking over the edge of the world.

As a relatively short loop it gives you the chance to get off the beaten track for a while, between blasting around the

Les Lindarets

Expert

Hard

12 km

230 m

775 m

2 hrs

IGN 3528
Morzine

trails at the new Châtel Bike Park. You could also use it to link through to the village of Châtel itself in order to sample some of the steep DH courses from the Super Châtel lift. Or you can use it to make up your own big XC loop around Châtel and the Val du Morgins.

Getting There

From Morzine and Les Gets

Most people will probably be approaching from this side of the mountain. To get to Les Lindarets, head for Montriond (D902 from Les Gets) and then take the smaller D228 towards Lac de Montriond. Pass the lake on the right, and continue up the mountain road to the village of Les Lindarets. Go through the small village (usually full of goats) and park at the bottom of the lift stations.

From the Châtel Valley.

If you are staying on the Châtel side of the mountain, head up the valley to Pre La Joux and take the Télésiège Pierres Longues to the mid station at Chalets La Praine Dranse and then continue to the top on the Plaine Dranse chair.

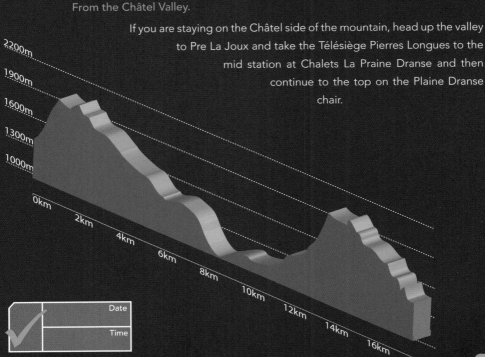

N

Très la Pierre

6

le Betzalin

5

Pré la Joux

Indu
wo

Small bike
park ramps

La Place
Des Plaines

4

GR5

1409

Télésiège de Pierre-Longue

les Grands
Plans

3

la Mouille
Ronde

1750

1616

1550

1950

D228

2

1778

1950

1

1750

les Lindarets

1750

Ardent

Télécabine d'Ardent

S

F

GR5

Télésiège de la Chaux Fleurie

Point
Chau

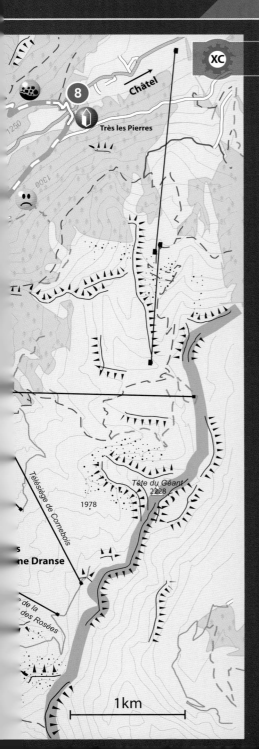

XC

Edge of the World Tour

Start Point

At the top of the lifts is the Crête Des Rochassons (Pt 1931m). Here the ground drops steeply away from you and the DH trails at the recently developed Châtel Bike Park on the Pre le Joux side of the valley seem to tumble directly off the side of the ridge. The Edge of the World ride starts more gently than this, following the 'Tour Panoramic' trail along the broad doubletrack to the left

Follow the VTT signs for the green 'Tour Panoramic' down a wide piece of newly cut singletrack. This speeds along skirting the contours of the west side of mountain just below the ridge line.

There are great views from here so remember to keep one eye on the trail if you're speeding along to make sure you don't whiz right off the mountain!

1 Signpost to Restaurant Le Bassachaux

At a small col at the end of the ridge the Tour Panoramic bends sharply round to the right and a narrow piece of singletrack carries straight on along the ridge line.

Go straight on here and onto the narrow shared use track (watch out for walkers) towards the resaurant. Follow this downwards, twisting and turning through the tree lined track and heather-filled narrow gullies. Pop out into the restaurant car park at Le Bassachaux with wonderful views down into the Châtel Valley.

2 Le Bassachaux Restaurant

Don't worry about the confusing signage here. Just head to the bottom of the car park to a panoramic view point and a map on a board and turn right.

Go down hill on the tarmac road for a short distance until you see a VTT sign on the Left. Go off the tarmac road on to a old water-worn fire track.

Look out for gullies and hidden rocks on this short technical section as come to some huts and on the edge of the woods.

3 Wide dirt track junction

Just near the collection of huts is a wide and slightly confusing track junction, go leftwards (go wrong and you'll end up back at the road) following signs to La Place des Plaines and Les Betzalin. Follow along a wooded and meadow section to a small wooden sign on your left.

Go straight on into the trees continueing toward Le Betzalin. Continue over a section prone to mud with water-worn gullies, using skill not to dab your feet.

4 La Place Des Plaines

At the junction in La Place Des Plaines, do not turn down hill, but stay on the left trail which takes you straight on through the meadow for a short uphill section. Go on through the woods on some mixed singletrack.

The trail starts innocently enough, gradually turning from broad bouncy doubletrack into narrowing singletrack. At a small picnic site the trail picks up speed, taking you into the woods and then heading slightly up hill. You'll need to muster all your skill to hop over roots and a few rocks here as there's a sheer drop to the right. Before you know it the track has narrowed to shoulders width and big hungry drops offs to the side have appeared.

Ride with caution on this section!.

You wouldn't want to fall off the side here, even with a few trees to break your slide. But ridden well, this is a thrilling and exhilarating section of genuinely testing singletrack. Keep your head for heights as you wiggle up and down traversing high above the valley rim.

5 Trail Junction / Stream

Arriving at a wide track and a stream you'll be genuinely grateful for the respite by now, but no doubt grinning like a cat that's got the cream. There is a small path continuing steeply down from here, but popular with walkers' it's best left alone. Head straight on along a wide forest track towards Le Betzalin.

6 Le Betzalin

Follow the road round to the left and back right at the buildings. Go through the meta bar gate and continue down a very old road which becomes overgrown and narrow Sweep down and round to the left until yo come into the woods.

The wide track now continues to skirt th valley and as you come out of the tree gives breathtaking views into the distanc mountains.

At a wide junction the trail suddenly veers steeply uphill to the GR5, with another trail heading off downhill in front of you. This is Sur Le Crac.

7 Junction / Sur le Crac (1460m)

Junction in trails signposted to Très Les Pierres. Going left will take you up hill for 200m if you fancy a steep climb on to join the GR5 trail but otherwise turn right here going between some large boulders.

Grab your wits and handlebars for a joint shaking steep ride following the very loose rocky track down hill. Don't hang on too tightly though, let those big forks do their work and you'll enjoy it all the more!

You gain a fair bit of speed here so look out for the 360 degree turn back right taking you down again steeply until the trail meets a small road. On the tarmac, turn left and follow speedily for a short distance to the main road.

8 Main Road / Très Les Pierres

At the junction here at the south end of Très Les Pierres, there is a large wooden signpost a. Cross the road here and turn to your right, riding for a very short distance until a left turn over a bridge takes you on to a well maintained fire track. Follow this immediately rightwards as it makes its way steadily uphill for a couple of kilometres.

9 Industrial Works

Don't take any right turns uphill until you cross a road over a stream by a small industrial works to the left. Keep straight on following the line of the river and passing a new small technical wooden ramps park to the right.

Ramps Park

Have a go on these, watching out you don't slip when they're wet, then carry on slightly up hill past interesting rocks and trees until the track finally reaches the main road again.

Pierre Longues Télécabine

Head up hill again for a hundred metres to the Pierre Longues télécabine and take this back up to Les Chalet De Plaines Dranse Here you can take in a few downhill runs at the Châtel Bike Park or go up again on the Teleseige de Rochassons to the peak above Les Lindetets.

Circuit of the Tête du Géant

Lindarets

Summary

For a good long day out amongst breathtaking alpine scenery this route is a must. Not only does it give your legs and lungs a good work out, it also gives you the opportunity to see what the whole area is made of. Take some money for an en-route stop at the Swiss mountain hut and restaurant at La Tovassiere and a chance to chill out in the peaceful alpine valley overlooking Morgins.

The ride starts off at the recently developed Châtel Bike Park, but quickly takes you away from the built trails into natural woodland and challenging little used trails. Dropping you suddenly out of the woods the route then deposits you at the start of the Morgins Valley. From here you wind ever upwards, with the impressive bulk of the Tête du Géant ever present in the distance.

Les Lindarets

One section of 4

Hard **3**

33 km

600 m

1750 m

4-6 hrs

IGN 3528 Morzine

Suisse Val D'Illez

Save some energy for after lunch and the last lung-busting ascent. You'll be glad you made the effort as you reach the Pas de Portes du Soleil and it's all spectacularly downhill from here. The only bit of 'up' from here on, involves the most impressive of all the lifts around these parts which takes you up to the Point des Mossetts.

Don't leave it too late in the day and you could also include some of the more remote DH riding at Les Crosets or sample some of the rides at the very recently opened Châtel Bike Park.

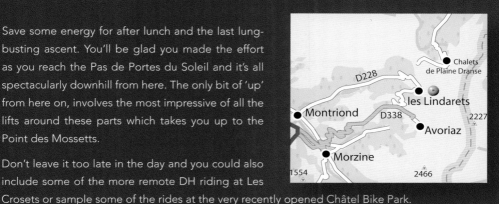

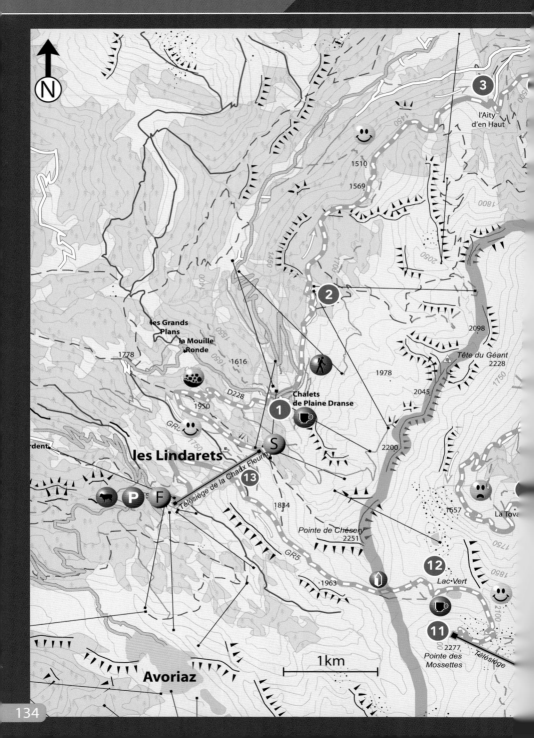

N

les Grands
Plans
la Mouille
Ronde

1778

les Lindarets

ardenti

D228

1616

1950

GR

1750

l'Aity
d'en Haut

3

1510

1569

2

2098

Tête du Géant
2228

1978

2045

2200

Chalets
de Plaine Dranse

1

S

13

Télésiège de la Chaux Fleurie

1884

Pointe de Chésery
2251

GR5

1963

2100

1657

La Tova

12

Lac Vert

1750

11

2277
Pointe des
Mossettes

Télésiège

P

F

Avoriaz

1km

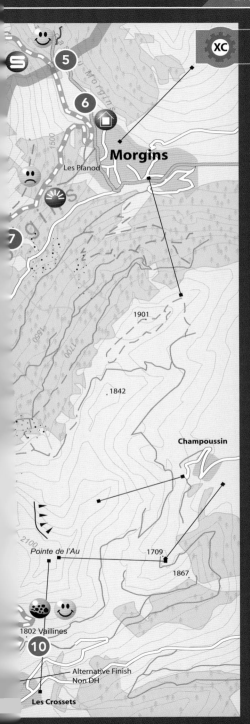

The Tête du Géant

Getting There

From Morzine and Les Gets -

Most people will probably be approaching from this side of the mountain. To get to Les Lindarets, head for Montriond (D902 from Les Gets) and then take the smaller D228 towards Lac de Montriond. Pass the lake on the right, and continue up the mountain road to the village of Les Lindarets. Go through the small village (always full of goats) and park at the bottom of the lift stations.

From the Châtel Valley -

If you are staying on the Châtel side of the mountain, head up the valley to Pre La Joux and take the Télésiège Pierres Longues to the mid station at Chalets La Praine Dranse.

Start Point

Park at Les Linderats and take the Télésiège de la Chaux Fleurie. At the top of the lift, turn left and follow 'Le Panoramic' down to the

mid station and a road head.

① Road Head

Go straight on past the collection of buildings to the road head. After the buildings go immediately right up a track (signed VTT Tour de Portes du Soleils). Continue along the track for about 1.5km until you descend slightly to a collection of lift stations.

2 Lift Stations

Go through the the collection of lift stations and directly ahead is a path going straight on and slightly uphill (signed VTT). Follow the path without any turnoffs, as it undulates enjoyably along pdirt singletrack. Go carefully along the section that was recently washed away by an avalanche! This spot gives vertiginous views down to the bottom of the valley.

Eventually the singletrack gives way and widens to a broad and steep track. As you hare downhill you pass a signpost at 1473m, and then come to an opening in the forest at L'Aity de'n Haut (1373m). Slow down as you approach L'Aity de'n Haut, as just before it is a path on the right (just on the side of a ski piste) going uphill. The path is signposted to 'Pas du Morgins and Pertuis en Bas'

3 L'Aity de'n Haut 1373m

Follow the path right towards the Pas du Morgins. After going uphill for 100m the path forks, go left, again following the sign to the Pas du Morgins. Push briefly up the muddy track and then get back on and ride as it levels off. The track continues muddily on for a while until you eventually come to a sweeping right hand bend and another sign.

At this point the track to the Pas du Morginss goes straight on along an overgrown grassy path. After a very short distance the track abruptly stops at a small rock bluff and seems to end. But appearing out of this is a small narrow trail and some of the craziest singletrack on the ride.

4 Start of Narrow Path

At the start the trail is literally just a foot wide, with big open drops off to the side. YES it really does go down there! So get concentrating and get ready to enjoy.

After a few hundred metres the drop on the left hand side doesn't seem quite so terrifying and the trail widens enough to put the feet back in the clips and to start to relax. Now the trail heads darkly into the trees. Pass a turn to the left and continue along the rooty path. The last few hundred metres are steep with lots of tight little switchbacks.

5 Pas du Morgins

Making your last switchback and dropping on to the road, you now have half the bike in France and half in Switzerland. No doubt grinning from ear to ear from the last bit of riding, chill for a minute at the lake, enjoy the views of the magnificent Dent Blanche mountains in the distance and then prepare yourself for a bit of easy re-ascent.

Go along the lane following the right hand side of the lake.

6 Farm & Large House

After a farm and then a large house, a small path goes up to the right (here there is a small innocuous VTT sign high up on a telegraph pole). Go along the path to a road junction. At the road turn right and follow the forest track around the hillside, where occasionally the trees part to give spectacular views of the Morgins valley and the Dent Blanche.

7 Track Junction 1533m

At a sweeping right hand bend near a farm, the trail continues straight on on grassy doubletrack (VTT sign again). Bounce amiably down the grassy track to finally arrive at a small road. Turn right and ramble your way upwards to the Restaurant La Tovassiere.

8 La Tovassiere 1689m

The friendly alpine restaurant here makes a great place to refuel before the final cruel bit of re-ascent. Leave the restaurant and head uphill behind the building (signed to Pas de Portes du Soleil).

The start is a hard steep and stony hill. Either engage superhuman thighs or be prepared for some short bouts of pushing. Just when you think that its all getting a bit tedious, the track eases off and you can start enjoying the riding again as it zigzags through pretty meadows, complete with alpine cows, bells and all.

9 Pas de Portes du Soleil.

At the pass is a small cross and a fantastic viewpoint and usually crowds of tourists. Go straight on at the top and head gratefully downhill towards Les Crosets. Hang on to your handlebars for a very fast descent.

10 Vaillane 1802m

At a junction turn right and traverse the hillside towards the telephrique. Just after going under the telephrique cables a downhill course goes off left to the lift station. Follow

can miss the DH course out by continuing to traverse around and down).

11 Les Crosets Lift

Take the Les Crosets lift up to the Point de Mossetts (2277m). This is the most spectacular lift around with steep jagged ridges and sheer mountains surrounding you. At the top follow the sign to the Lac Verte and the Col de Chésery. Although wide the track starts off steep, stony and technical with big rocks all around. Gradually it eases into a flowing track as it enters the bowl and sweeps past the Lac Verte.

12 Lac Verte 1981m

At a small teahouse follow the track rightwards (No Bikes sign straight on) and take a slight detour to the Col de Chésery. At the col, follow signposts to Les Lindarets. This is the GR5, one of Europe's networks of long distance footpaths and seems to be popular both with alpine cows and with long distance walkers - watch out for both! This is a fun rutted dirt trail with lots of lines to choose from. Continue on to the pistes of Les Lindarets.

13 Les Lindarets

When you arrive at the piste fences, follow signs or choose one of the DH courses to get back to your car.

Depending on time, either go down to the village and photograph the famous goats or head back up on the lifts for a quick DH hit on the Châtel side of the mountain.

Les Crosets

Getting There

The routes at Les Crosets can be accessed
from Avoriaz. To do this; take the Télésiège
des Brochaux from Avoriaz and then
the Mossettes Lift up to the Pointe des
Mossettes. From here you will need to ride
down to the bottom of the Les Crosets lift.

If you are staying over on the Champery
side of the mountain, then getting to this
ride is much easier, with a short journey up
to the village of Les Crosets to start.

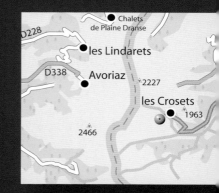

Start Point

From Les Crosets take the lift on the Champery side of the village. When at the top turn t

he Swiss National

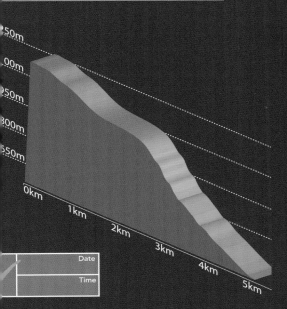

250m
00m
950m
800m
550m

0km
1km
2km
3km
4km
5km

| | Date |
| | Time |

Les Crosets

Downhill — DH

Extreme — 4

5 km

600 m

10 -30 mins

IGN 3528
Morzine

he Shorty

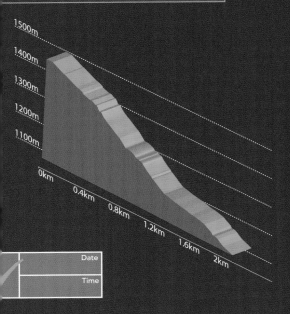

1500m
1400m
1300m
1200m
1100m

0km
0.4km
0.8km
1.2km
1.6km
2km

| | Date |
| | Time |

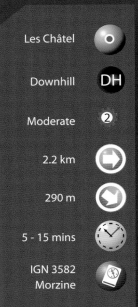

Les Châtel

Downhill — DH

Moderate — 2

2.2 km

290 m

5 - 15 mins

IGN 3582
Morzine

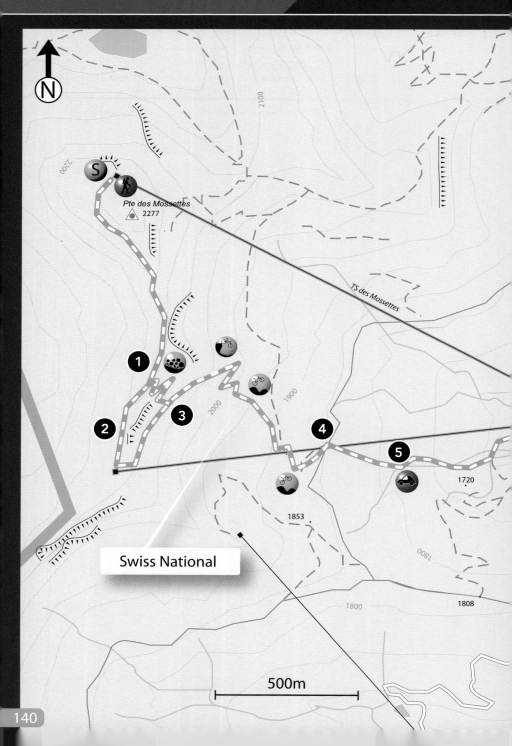

Pte des Mossettes
2277

TS des Mossettes

Swiss National

500m

les Crossets

DH Summary: The Swiss National

With a fair amount of concentration, this track can be rolled down , but to get the most from the Swiss national track, you will need to be good through corners and confident about jumping.

The start is a long track, starting with a newly cut, steeply cornered rocky section. After this fairly short section the track opens up a bit more and becomes faster with bigger jumps. As you progress downwards, the ride continues to get faster and the jumps larger.

There are still some tight corners further down the track and these need to be railed at full speed if you want to clear the jumps.

DH Summary: The Shorty

The Les Crosets 'Shorty' is a moderately compact track with a lot of fun packed into a small space. It makes an entertaining trail to section over and over, as it includes quite a mixed bag and doesn't take long to get up and down several times.

The track starts off with some fast straights, some big open corners and some trickily placed tight corners. As you get further down to the bottom the straight sections get shorter and the steep sections get steeper.

Use it as a warm up for the B1 or just enjoy it for itself.

The Swiss National

① Start 1

Start No 1 begins with a series of tight s-bends interspersed with small jumps and weaving corners. A couple of really tight corners before two fairly long flat sections, then a tight left where you meet up with the other section.

② Start 2

At this optional start point you begin the ride with a short section of narrow singletrack down to a fire road. Turn left then left again and head down the long straight track. The trail weaves from side to side with jumps and small wall rides in between.

③ Weaving Track

The weaving track continues on a loose surface into a tight right. This is where you start to get a feel for the rest of the track. A very steep s-bend section opens up over a small jump, take a slight left, a tighter right and over a fairly large step down.

This is roll-able at a slower speed and on the right hand side. Do the jump and you will carry a lot of speed onto the following bumpy straight and awkward lump before a right-hander takes you into more tight s-bends.

Round a big left hand wall ride, a slight right and another large step down. Slightly larger this time but again roll-able on the right hand side. Get some speed here for the slight uphill and round a hut to your right.

④ Gap Jump

If you like jumps have a go at the fairly large gap jump but you need to be shifting. This i roll able at slower speeds. A slight left int more tight s-bends including a rocky section takes you left onto a small straight with a hip able left.

Steep shoot into s-bends on the exit of the left-hander. There is a huge gap (roll-able into a left and smallish double and slightl larger tabletop. Turn left on the road and the track continues about fifty metres furthe down on the right.

⑤ Road

Turn right off the road, go slightly right again and then ther is a really fun section of track A long straight with lots of small gap jump (all roll-able) across a bridge and huge lef wall ride.It all gets narrow for a second with a slight right through some trees, then more s bends follow. These are not to close togethe and interspersed with small jumps and ther get tighter taking you into a fairly steep rolle coaster section.

On the exit of the last left there is a large roac gap (roll-able to the right) and then a couple more jumps to the finish.

The Shorty

Metal Cattle Bridge

art over a narrow metal cattle bridge and
on pick up speed down the first straight
nto the flat section and into the first right.
areful as you go over the crest, as there is
tight left-hander to catch you out. Then it's
.o a series of tight s-bends and onto a small
raight with a flattish left right at the end.
nother fast straight, a left and then a small
mp onto a rocky section.

om here go round an easy open left-hander
nd onto a straight with more scattered rocks
llowed by a slight right down to some trees
nd a big right just as you think your heading
ght into the trees.

Another fast straight takes you into a sligh
left/right kink and some roots and then into
a rocky off camber left. Follow this with a
steep right onto some nice tight singletrack
with a left/right to take you into some trees
Next, some fairly open s-bends lead to sma
straight which drops down to a tight but fas
right-hander.

2 Wooden Bridge

A short straight leads over small wooder
bridge into trees and onto some steep tight s-
bends. This opens up over some nice weaving
rooty single-track with a couple more steep
s-bends through more trees and you're ou
into the open, only a short flat section away
from the finish.

bikefax

Summary

Kate's 'Big Day Out' is an awesome combinatin of amazing open views and sumptuous singletrack. Entertainingly bringing together stunning down hill sections, fast fire-roads and highly technical steep-sided slopes, this ride is set to delight the trail hungry adventurer.

The route starts by taking a ride on the Télésiège Des Mossettes, one of the steepest and most exposed lifts around. The long lift takes about 25mins to ascend, and can get pretty cold as you approach the top which is so often in the cloud s. If you're lucky, and it's a cloud free day, you'll get to see some of the most amazing views in the area with jagged peaks and tree-lined ridges surrounding you on all sides.

Take everything you need to be self sufficient for the day and check lift times before you set off.

Télésiège des Mossettes

Classic

Hard

32 km

270 m

1390 m

4.5 hrs

IGN 3528 Morzine

Getting There

For the full day out start from Pointe Des Mossettes which you can reach from the Télésiège de s Mossettes (a little further east of Les Lindarets) or the Les Crosets lift on the Châtel side of the hill.

It is possible to join this trail at Montriond, Morzine, Avoriaz, Les Lindarets or Le Crête Des Rochassons and you can lift hop all the way from Les Gets.

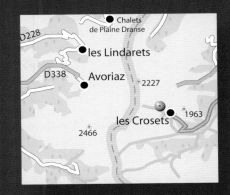

Start Point

Start the route at the top of the Télésiège des Mossettes.

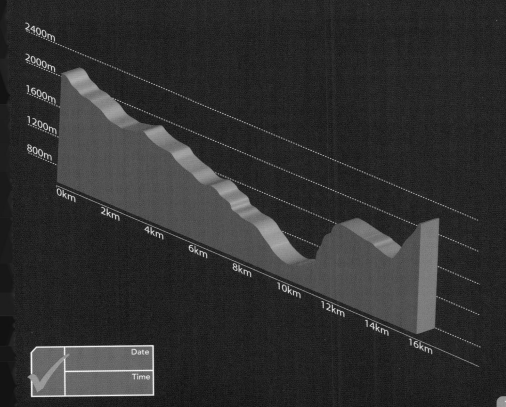

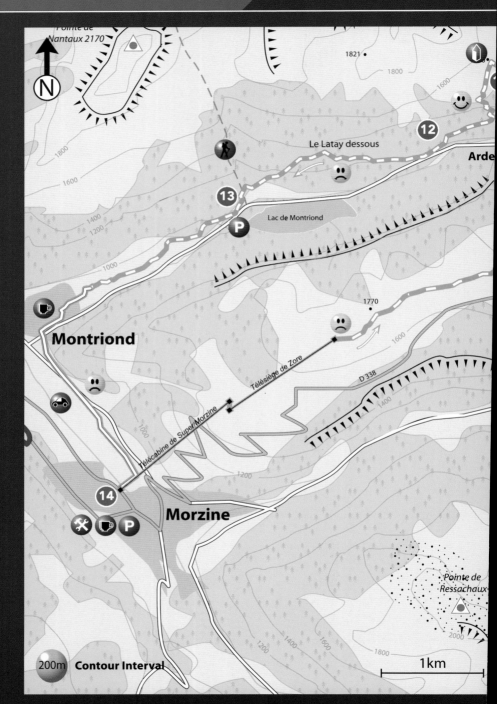

N

Pointe de
Nantaux 2170

1821 •

1800

1600

1600

1800

Le Latay dessous

12

Arde

1600

13

1400
1200

P

Lac de Montriond

1000

1770

Montriond

Télésiège de Zore

D 338

1400

Télécabine de Super Morzine

1000

1200

1600

14

Morzine

Pointe de
Ressachaux

2000

1200

1400

1600

1800

2000

200m **Contour Interval**

1km

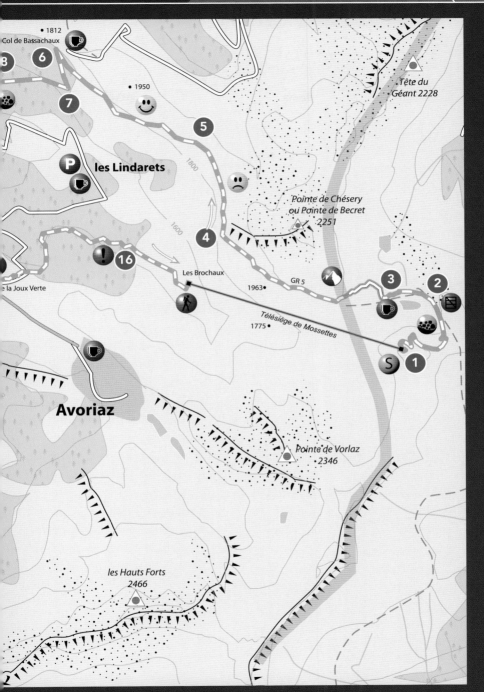

• 1812
Col de Bassachaux

les Lindarets

• 1950

Tête du
Géant 2228

Pointe de Chésery
ou Pointe de Becret
2251

Les Brochaux

GR 5

1963•

Télésiège de Mossettes

1775•

e la Joux Verte

Avoriaz

Pointe de Vorlaz
2346

les Hauts Forts
2466

Kate's Big Day Out

(1) Point des Mossettes

At the Point Des Mossettes (2277m) look down the track from the path between the two lift stations and roll down to the sign post which includes an arrow for Tour de Portes du Soleil VTT .

Follow the track either straight down a steep slope or around to the left with a right turn to quite quickly to join up with the fire track. This is wide and open at the start but steepens and narrows quite quickly to zig zag down to what's known as: 'puncture alley' for obvious reasons.

The trail is very fast with loose rocks in abundance so check your brakes and dont be afraid to pause. Dont feel the need for heroics, many a person has crashed and burned here!!

(2) Cattle grid junction

At a junction of fire roads separated by electric fencing, catch your breath and fix any punctures before turning left and following the VTT sign.

Before you move on, check out the truly amazing alpine views. Looking to the left side of the ridge ahead you'll get a great view of the GR5, an international long distance trail, which skirts along where you're heading over to next by following a gracefully winding track.

(3) Lac Coffee Refuge

When you reach the Tour de VTT sign at a small lake at Chésery Pt1981m, either stop for a coffee at the mountain refuge where there's a warm welcome or carry on along rough singletrack. Pass to the right of the hut, trying not to look too out of control as you struggle to keep your balance on the uneven ground.

Do not be tempted to go to the left of the hut where there's a 'no bikes' sign as this does not maintain your height (or the respect of the hut guardian!) and the terrain is no better than the next section.

After coming over a small rise and following the track for a short distance. The trail joins some faster and easier single-track. Turn left at the VTT sign to go along more open undulating trail to a junction where you follow the signs to Montriond.

A short section of water worn trail then rises up slightly and leads you on to a fast technical singletrack. At the 'Tour VTT Portes de Soleil ' sign, take the right fork . After a 100 metres turn left where tarmac then turns into fast rocky fire road running to the right of the river. Pop out on to a road for 10 metres and then on then right again to follow a red VTT sign and a footpath sign to Bravachet 995m and Montriond.

(4) GR5 junction

At a fork in the trail, take the right turn off for the GR5 and a steep uphill section on worn singletrack. Look out for people riding down in the opposite direction. Normally the left fork would take you down a fast and interesting path all the way to the bottom, skirting under the lift before reaching the car park, but at the time of writing due to the building of a new road from Les Lindarets over to Les Crosets, the right fork is a better options.

5 View of Pre La Joux

At the top lift station at Les Lindarets take in the view of the Pre Le Joux bike park then head left. Follow the tall metal VTT sign posted trail down left which descends back on to the GR5 for a short distance rising up in a quick stretch running you parallel with and underneath the start section of the new green tour Panoramic.

Come to the Col de Bassachaux restaurant car park at 1800m where, in the restaurant, there is a great lunch to be had if your timing is right.

The signage and layout of the car park is confusing so go to the left straight away here following the VTT sign (amongst walkers sign posts) pointing to les Lindarets.

6 Bum slide

On a great piece of wide worn trail here wiggle around a few corners looking out on the water worn surface for drainage ditches. This track takes you round to the right becoming narrower up to a VTT sign to the left. Take this turn down on to a newly cut, slippery and very steep slope (which either has you hanging well over the back of your seat or hopping off your bike briefly) bringing you into the woods. After a short rooty section, and as the track becomes more rocky, watch out for a big right hand turn. Speed over another short big-root section then down a wide gravely fire track to a junction in trails.

7 Junction uphill

At this junction, take the right hand trail which leads uphill on old singletrack. This track narrows quickly uphill to make you muster your technical prowess up through a steep muddy rise in a clearing. Look out for the owners of the many hoof prints here!

Keep on up hill, bearing round to the left slightly and coming between the valleys, until you reach an open meadow and a wooden sign.

8 Avalanche sign

At an avalanche warning sign, plus several wooden signs right in the middle of the grassy meadow all pointing to Col de Brassachaux, go back the way you came to les Lindarets and then off to the left.

Take the left turn. This takes you past a technical rocky section before coming into the trees. After crossing a stream, tackle a quick rise on to lovely, sparsely used singletrack.

9 Tin roof with a view

The trail brings you to another avalanche sign and a wooden sign pointing back the way you came to Col de Bassachaux. In a steep-sided high grassy meadow, begin to use your balancing skills on wonderful off camber narrow trail bringing you through some trees and past a little wooden hut with a metal roof.

10 Slippery wood

Heading into the trees now, you run down below the left of a rocky outcrop. This section is steep and needs your entire technical prowess, but it is a real stunner. Zig zagging down through the woods now and passing some amazing old trees you're on some of the best singletrack around.

Wooden signposts here point down to Ardent and Montriond with one pointing back up to Les Lindarets. Deceptively slippery wooded section here where you're much better ON your bike than OFF it. Watch your braking especially on the corners as there are some steep slopes below.

11 Metal pipe and Manger

As you keep heading down, look out for a tricky raised metal pipe on the trail. Just after this, come down to the right over a rocky and rooty section to wriggle past another metal avalanche sign.

Heading through the fantastic old woods now pass a wooden hay manger for goats.

A foot path sign at1260m points you back up to les Lindarets, straight down to Les Choseau, Lac de Montriond and a pretty waterfall Cascade D'Ardent. Take the track to keep your height here going toward le Latay dessous.

12 Stay high

Right turn keep higher up in the woods on lovely undulating singletrack with some short bursts of technically taxing uphill. Keep going until you get to La Maison L'Neuve.

Choose to turn down here to the road popping out by a great hotel restaurant called L'Auberge de Derdoyant or carry straight on to skirt along narrow undulating singletrack over some roots ignoring the turns down to the left until you reach the small group of houses at Le Latay Dessous.

This brings you along a lovely wooded trail which joins up with the main road by turning down sharply for the last 100m. Follow the trail as it turns down to the left and brings you to the main road near the end of Lac de Montriond with the Spa back on your left.

13 Montriond

Turn right for a short tarmac section on the flat, until a fork in the road. Take the right fork with the road sign to 'Dranse de Morzine'. Quickly follow the VTT signs which weave in and out of the trees and road to the right of the river.

When you come back on the road at a fork with a bridge over the river, turn left over the bridge for a short ascent which brings you to the middle northern side of Montriond. Heading rightward on the main road and right again at the mini round about, stay on this road through town all the way back to the metal walkers bridge bringing you to the bottom of the Télécabine de Super Morzine.

14 Lift rest

Have a rest on the lift as it takes you back up most of the slope. On leaving this lift, look right and roll down to a smaller chair lift which takes you to the very top. Its a bit colder up here, so keep up your momentum by heading straight out to your right and up the fire road shared by slow cars.

After undulating upward for a short while, playing on the small worn wall rides in the bank to your left, top out at a closed lift station.

At the split in trails ahead, take the middle line and enjoy a short section of rooty mixed terrain singletrack. Stay straight on past a large wooden walkers sign when you can see the road to your right. A similarly mixed short section now brings you to a steep slope down on to a main road junction by a large road sign.

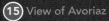 **View of Avoriaz**

At the road junction, look over to your right for a view of the strange wooden town of Avoriaz on the horizon.

Look right now to a small VTT sign which drops you off the road on to a twisting fast down hill section. Look out for DH boys and girls, as this allthough this is their cut through from

Morzine to Les Lindarets, the trail is shared by all and sundry. Where the trail brings you back out on to the road, head off to the right down a wide rooty earthy track where you can pick up some real speed for a quick rise straight on (not left) at a junction in trails.

 Speeding home

Now just keep on going, as the track narrows along fast undulating ground. Look out for a taped off section. This is where the trail crosses the French National track at Les Lindarets. Its worth a stop to look up right and watch some loonies fly down the incredibly steep slopes which dropp off down to your left.

Head on from here and go straight on skirting into the woods again with some slight uphill, which finally brings you come out of the vegetation and into the open. Head left and drop down an open slope to Les Brochaux ready to take the Télésiège des Mossettes back to the start.

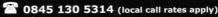

French National Downhill Course

Avoriaz

Summary

This particularly fierce track, was used in 2005 for a round of the French Nationals, hence the name. The track requires the utmost attention at all times.

There are very few places for a mental rest and none for a physical moment off. From rocks to huge drops, from big gaps to flat out rough open corners, this track has it all.

The French National is one of the few official trails in an otherwise very rocky area. In our view, it makes a very welcome addition to the already fantastiv network of tracks in the region.

Go and try it, but be prepared!

Les Lindarets

Downhill **DH**

Off the scale **5**

3.8 km

350 m

5 mins - 1 hr!

IGN Morzine 3528

Getting there

If you've got a car, drive round to the village of Les Lindarets via Montriond and the Lac de Montriond. There is plenty of parking at hte bottom hte lift stations.

OR

If you are carless, you can catch the Super Morzine lift nd the Telesiege La Zore to the top of the mountain. From here, follow the track to the Col de Joux Verte and then the minor road into Avoriaz.

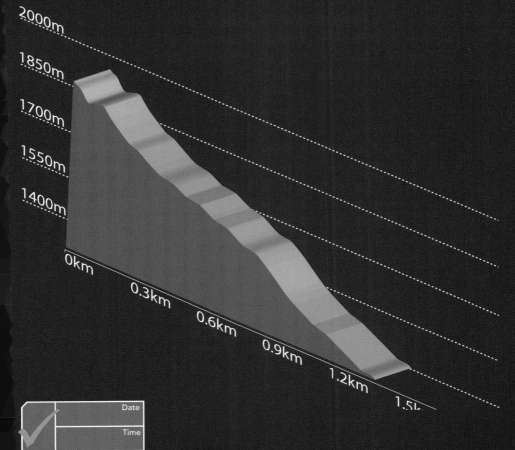

	Date
	Time

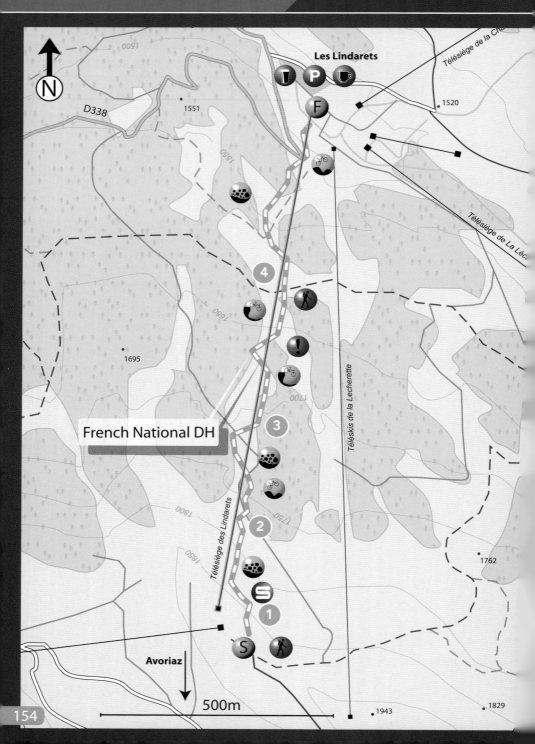

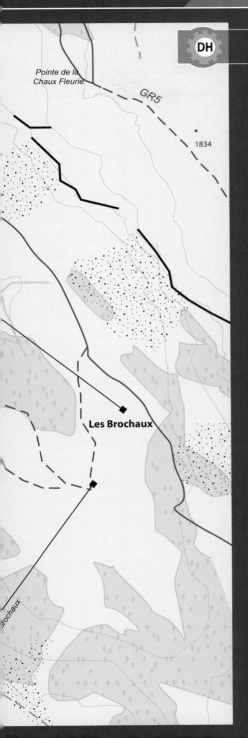

DH

The French National DH

Starting Point

From the main hub of Les Lindarets, head up the road in the direction of Avoriaz. When you reach the next cluster of cafes and the two lifts, you need to take the lift which heads up to Avoriaz.

At the top of this lift take the fire road which heads off on your far left down the hill. After a few hundred metres the track starts on your left.

1 Start of track

The track starts by dropping off the side of the fire-road into a series of tight steep s-bends, going right, left, then right again. Then some steep corners with two right left combo's. These open up and get more bumpy and rough takin you onto a small straight. Be careful over the crest, as on the other side is a very tight right left, then another right over a crest again.

This is where it starts to get rocky, so be aware. The trail straightens up here and goes up and over little crests with small turns each way. Despite the rocks, this section flows incredibly well and once you can anticipate what is coming is very enjoyable.

The trail then heads left towards a big rock, and as you get to it the trail bends right round to the right then down and over a smaller rock to a crossing.

Pointe de la
Chaux Fleurie

GR5

1834

Les Brochaux

2 Tricky Trees

Then it's into the woods for the first time, and round a big tree on the left into a very tricky section. Either take the pro line to the left with a blind jump into a very narrow gap onto rocks or, the right line through a rocky little gully.

After that there is a right turn with either a rock line on the right or a slower smoother line on the left, taking you into a rutty right. From here its into a very rocky left before a slightly less rocky right to small drop and larger drop. Both of these drops can be rolled round to left hand side.

After the drops you pick up a bit of speed down a fast shoot. You need this speed to get up the following tricky rock section. The best line for this short section of uphill is to take the smooth rocks to the left hand side and then left around the tricky tree at the top.

Then a small fairly open s-bend section into another tight corner to the right round another tree. More rocks to the right hand side or a smoother line down the left take you into more rocks through more trees.

Turning right onto possibly the rockiest section of all, which together with some roots, makes the left at the bottom of the little shoot very hard to get round with any dignity. Jump over a rock to the right or roll round to the left to get to the next stage.

3 Beware! Big Drop!

A small left onto a fast straight is no let up as you go round a slight right to reveal two lines, jumps on the right hand side. The two lines meet back up again for a quite tight right round a tree to a fast chute and a slight left over a drop onto rocks.

BEWARE, Big drop ahead, This can be rolled on the very left but it is still quite steep.

The drop is around 2 metres in height depending where you land but the landing is only short or it is onto the flat. After this is a bit of a right, depending on how you take the drop, then onto a really fast section with lots of small rocks and a vague right left s-bend, then suddenly a super tight right around a tree.

Now there are three lines to choose from. The first; the pro line, is a very sharp left through a large split between two rocks with a very tricky exit at the end. The second line is a less sharp left and round the outside of the rocks, this meets up with line one and turns right to a route crossing. Line three misses out the little section altogether and just goes straight to the route crossing.

4 The Pro Line

The pro line from here is straight on and jumps the drop to land near the flat at the bottom. There are 3 other options available, first, do the drop but just roll down - taking care to slow down in time for the corner at the bottom. Second, there is a less steep chute round to the right, or third option there is a really easy bit of singletrack about 20-25 metres to the right hand side but this miss's out quite a large section of the main trail. From one of the first 2 options, take the left after the drop, with care as you do pick up a lot of speed.

This takes you to a rocky little straight with a tight right hairpin followed by a left right combo. Round to the right and you are faced immediately with a quite large step down, which can be rolled, or there is chicken run round to the right.

Either way, you pick up speed for a slightly off camber left in the open where it is easy to drift off the track, but you are on the open piste so it is not so important. Here you need all the speed you can find to get up the little bank in front of you. There is a little ditch in the way, which needs to be hopped to keep the speed up. Once over the bank, go round a long right, to a small straight (here you are zig zaging across the piste) with a small but tricky stream jump at the end (this is roll-able to the right hand side but quite rocky).

Fly over the crest, following with a right-hander and on towards another small stream jump. This time the jump in is on the right, but the landing is uphill and not very nice (rollable to the left). A big open right to a tighter left and a small gap (a lot nicer than the others) takes you to the right (or roll left).

Then it is all out to pedal to the finish round a small right and to a big gap. This is a flat lander if not jumped far enough. Jump this far and you will need to give it a bit of right hand hip also. This is the end of the course - you can breath again now.

Pedal to the finish.
Relax!

Lift Information

Summer opening times

Avoriaz 26 June to 28 August	
Télésiège de Super Morzine	9.30 am - 5.15 pm
Des Lindarets	9.30 am - 5.15 pm
Des Mossettes	9.45 am - 4.45 pm
De Zore	9.30 am - 5.15 pm
Champerey 12 June to 23 October	
Telepherique Champery-Planachaux:	8.30 am - 5.30 pm
Les Crossets 2nd July to 28 August.	
Télésiège Crosets – Point de Mossettes	9.00 am - 5.00 pm
Télésiège Crosets II	9.00 am - 5.00 pm
Champoussin 2 July to 21 August	
Télésiège Aiguille des Champeys	10.00 am- 4.00 pm
Châtel 24 June 4 September	
Télécabine de Super Châtel	9.00 am - 5.30 pm
Télésiège du Morclan	9.00 am - 5.00 pm
Télésiège de Pierre Longue	9.00 am - 5.00 pm
Télésiège des Rochassons	9.00 am - 5.00 pm
Les Gets 7June to 11September	
Télécabine des Chevannes	9.30 am - 5.30 pm
Télécabine du Mont Chéry	9.30 am - 5.30 pm
Télécabine de la Pointe	9.45 am - 4.45 pm
Morgins 25 June to 28th August	
Télésiège la Foilleuse	10.00 am -5.00 pm
Morzine 4th June to 11th September	
Télécabine du Pleney	9.30 am - 6.00 pm
Télésiège de la Crusaz	
Télésiège de la Pointe de Nyon	9.30 am - 5.00 pm
Montriond 24 June to 28 August	
Télésiège de Chaux Fleurie	9.30 am - 4.30 pm
Télésiège des Lindarets	10.00 am 5.00 pm
Télésiège des Mossettes	10.00 am- 4.00 pm

If you're planning on heading off the beaten track, keep an eye on the lift times, especially towards the end of the season when things start to close down early.

Prices at the time of writing are around 14 euro per day or 48 euro per week or, if you're staying for more than 3 weeks, a season pass can be the most economical purchase at 110 euro. Just try not to lose it!! If you do, and it is one with a photograph on, there will be a record of it at the lift station where you purchased it, so don't despair.

DH

XC

Acknowledgments

A big thank you is due to the local French Councils and Portes du Soleil Tourist Board together with their Promotions Officer and everyone else who puts their hard work into creating and maintaining the trails and lifts for us summer visitors. Without these organisations this book would not have been inspired.

Thanks a million to Craig, Rich, Mark, Anthony and all from Ride On. Big snogs to Rich for all his trail advice and Craig for use of brilliant Giants and photos. Ride On's mechanical knowledge and use of workshop proved invaluable yet again. Thanks too to Pete for long loan of a GPS, which was immeasurably helpful.

Thanks to JM and everyone at The Boomerang for another great summer with them and especially to Jed and Ben for NOT feeding me 'Ricard' this year!
Not forgetting the office team, this book would definitely not be here but for Chris Havills amazing hard work and undying attention to detail on the graphics side, Carwyn for his last minute help plus Sue and Jim's original enthusiasm, trails input and continued support throughout. Once again thanks to Jim for his ceaseless trail energy. Sadly this time Welly didnt have his passport in order and had to stay at home.

Thanks to Fabien Barel, Ben Gaby, and Rus Carty at Kona for their support.

Finally, thanks to Krien Dawson form Vario fc lending Chris the deceptively good Kaktus an the ever grinning Dan White from Royal fc wardrobe assistance!
You're all brilliant. Thanks!

Photographs:

Kate Long, Chris Lazenby, Craig Robertson, Dan Croft, Sue Savege, Jim Savege